CLASSICBEER **1** ST

D0195661

PALE ALE

BY TERRY FOSTER

A Brewers Publications Book

Pale Ale
By Terry Foster, Ph.D.
Classic Beer Style Series
Edited by Laura Allbritten
Copyright 1990 by Terry Foster

ISBN 0-937381-18-7
Printed in the United States of America
10 9 8 7 6

Published by Brewers Publications,
a division of the Association of Brewers Inc.
PO Box 1679, Boulder, Colorado 80306-1679 USA
(303) 447-0816 • FAX (303) 447-2825

Direct all inquiries/orders to the above address.

Cover design by Robert L. Schram
Cover photograpy by Michael Lichter, Michael Lichter Photography
Darts courtesy of Leisure Time Products, Boulder, Colo.

Table of Contents

Acknowledgements

Brewers Publications would like to thank these companies and individuals for letting us use the following photography and/or artwork in this book:

English Hops Ltd.; page 47.
Terry Foster, author; pages 77, 83.
Merchant du Vin; pages 7, 14, 20, 27.
Charlie Papazian, Association of Brewers; pages 68, 105, 109, 125.
Samuel Smith, The Old Brewery, Tadcaster; pages 11, 73.
Young's Brewery; pages 32, 41.

About the Author

Born and bred in London, Terry Foster has lived in the United States for the last 12 years and has experienced both the British and the American homebrewing "revolutions." He holds a Ph.D. in chemistry (London University) and is a Principal Scientist in an international technical service group of a major mining chemicals manufacturer. He travels extensively and enjoys tasting the beers of other countries.

Foster has been brewing for thirty years and has written extensively on a number of brewing topics: beer history, beer styles, brewing chemistry and techniques, and commercial breweries. His articles have appeared in *England's Amateur Winemaker, The Amateur Brewer* (now *American Brewer*), *Home Fermenter's Digest*, and **zymurgy**. Foster published *Dr. Foster's Book of Beer* (now out of print) in England in 1978. He loves Fuller's London Pride, Altbier, Anchor Liberty Ale, New England seafood, and the Boston Red Sox. His hates include "lite" beers, fast foods, and the Yankees.

Introduction

What was your first brew? It is a good bet that, like many homebrewers, you started with a version of pale ale. One of the reasons for doing so is that this is a major beer style in anybody's book. This book's aim is to look at what makes pale ale so important, and to show how to brew a variety of examples of the style, on both the home- and the microbrewery scale.

To do this properly, it will be necessary to differentiate between pale ale, bitter, and India pale ale, the last two being important subcategories of the style. This will require definitions of these beers in terms of brewing ingredients and procedures, analysis, flavor spectrum, and storage and serving methods.

Purely technical specifications are not enough, however. Any truly great beer has an indefinable quality reflecting the brewer's art (as opposed to his craft), his culture, and that of the people who drink the beer. To fully define pale ale we must also consider its history, who makes it, who drinks it and where they drink it.

My particular interest in pale ale is that I love to drink it! I am often asked "What is your favorite beer?" For the true beer-lover, as beer authority Michael Jackson points out, there is no one answer to this question since there are many factors which determine beer choice. However, if I were to be stranded on a desert island with only one beer, it would have to be a pale ale. Which one? Fuller's London Pride, of course. Or their ESB, or Young's Special, Greene King's Abbot Ale, Hook Norton Best Bitter, Taylor's Landlord, Adnam's Extra, Marston's Pedigree . . . .

In some countries, when a boy reaches a certain age it is customary for his father to take him to a bordello so as to ensure his proper initiation into one of life's greatest pleasures. In England the equivalent custom is for the father to take his son on his first visit to a pub and to supervise his initiation into the ritual of beer-drinking in a proper social environment. Such was my rite of passage, and the first beer my father bought for me was a pale ale. Fittingly, the first piece of writing I ever had published was an article on Worthington White Shield, a bottled pale ale of impeccable pedigree.

Pale ale is brewed in a number of countries, notably Scotland and Wales, as well as Belgium, the United States, Canada, Australia, South Africa and even tiny Malta. But it is quintessentially an English beer. England is where it originated and where by far the greatest volume of it is produced today.

For thousands of years beers were brewed only by top fermentation. Yet in little more than a hundred years it has been replaced by the bottom-fermentation method in most countries of the world. Pale ale, in terms of both quantity and variety, is the most important top-fermented beer style left and the greatest obstacle to domination of the beer world by lager styles.

In contrast to U.S. citizens, the English don't drink much beer at home. They prefer the pub—that most relaxed, convivial and invitingly social drinking establishment. It can offer conversation, games, meeting places for sports and other clubs, some of the best and cheapest food available in the country and sometimes comfortable accommodations. It has its roots in the private house where the owner sold the beer (or rather ale) which he brewed on the premises. At its best it is still simply an extension of the licensee's own house. The word "pub" can be found in bar names around the world, from America to Zambia, but only in England can the true pub atmosphere be found. Perhaps this has something to do with the English taking their progress slowly and making sure that they have kept the good from the past before throwing out the bad.

In fact, that is a rosy and oversentimental view. Both the English pub and pale ale are under siege; pale ale is at serious risk of disappearing entirely. Despite CAMRA's (Campaign for Real Ale) much-praised success, only 15 percent of 1988's total production consisted of traditional, cask-conditioned ale, although more than 80 percent of Britain's beer is sold on draught. About half the market is now lager beer, and its consumption still seems to be increasing. Worse yet, much of this lager is expensive, weak and lacking in flavor. How can I describe to you the anguish of an exile returning to England in search of the perfect pint of bitter, only to find the pubs full of bland lagers with pseudo-German names, and Budweiser, Miller, and Foster's everywhere?

Internal accounting pressures on the Big Six brewers (Bass, Allied Breweries, Whitbread, Watney, Courage, and Scottish & Newcastle) have pushed them to maximize returns from their large holdings of retail outlets. This means they have closed or sold off many pubs, often with a covenant barring their further use as pubs. Others have been converted into "theme" bars, restaurants or even discos. A marketing survey published in January 1989 by Mintel Publications suggests that an additional 5,000 pubs must soon close, and further states that a large proportion of the rest can only survive by becoming cafés and brasseries.

There is still hope, though. Pubs have always been subject to evolution and change because they have to satisfy the needs of a changing culture. The good pubs are those which have evolved slowly, taking account of those needs, yet retaining the things which first made them good pubs. Surely these will continue to survive, adapting a little, yet without changing their basic nature.

The survival of pale ale may still be in question. But it will be helped by the continuing efforts of CAMRA and those individuals who refuse to let a great beer be supplanted by a mediocre one. We can help the cause of pale ale both by drinking it and brewing it as much as possible. If this book encourages you to do so, then the effort of writing it will have been more than worthwhile!

1

History

The introduction of some beers, notably porter and Pilsener, can be traced fairly precisely. In the case of pale ale the very name is misleading. It was never pale in color, and it was probably first produced at a time when it would not have been called ale. That is because "ale" originally referred to an unhopped malt beverage, while one of the outstanding characteristics of this style is its high hop bitterness.

Other things about its origin are obscure, largely because it evolved in a time when there were few written records, and when most brewing in England was carried out in the home or in brewpubs rather than by wholesale brewers. In those times, little was understood about the true nature of the brewing process. The nature and function of yeast were still mysteries, and instruments such as the hydrometer and thermometer had not been introduced.

In order to understand the evolution of pale ale, it is necessary to consider the more general history of English brewing. Hops, and therefore beer, were introduced to England by Flemish migrants around 1500. The hop flavor of beer represented a major change in the taste of the nation's beverage. Since it was a foreign import and the preservative qualities of hops enabled unscrupulous brewers to sell a weaker product at the same price, it was a considerable time before beer replaced ale entirely.

By about the beginning of the 17th century it seems that beer had largely displaced ale as the drink of the common man. However, most of the great houses and mansions had their own breweries. These were often of fairly large capacity, for they supplied beer to both family and servants, and consumption levels were much higher than nowadays.

Many of these breweries continued to brew very strong, unhopped, long-matured ales. These were drunk from small, ornate glasses, often etched with barley motifs. The custom of brewing such ales probably died out in the first half of the 18th century as they lost their fashionable status to more exotic drinks such as tea and coffee. Also, many of the big houses ceased to do their own brewing during this period, for economies of scale made it cheaper to buy from the rapidly growing number of brewers.

As ale disappeared for good, its name came back into circulation and was applied to both dark and pale beers to distinguish them from porters and stouts. Pale beers had been around for a long time already, for the Burton pale style is recorded as having been on sale in London as far back as 1630. Burton, of course, is the town most people consider to be the home of the finest pale ales. Ironically, the more typical Burton style, as pointed out by Michael Jackson among others, was a dark, nut-brown beer. Such beers were still sold in England in the 1950's, under the simple name "Burton."

In 1760, a pseudonymous letter to a London magazine states that pale ales were introduced to the city by the

Delivering the ale.

"Gentry," who were habituated to them in the country. It is not entirely clear what he meant by the term pale ale, which was not yet a distinct style. What is clear is that the ordinary populace was drinking porter, partly because pale ale was too expensive for them. The relatively crude techniques of the time made it difficult to produce pale malt, so that it was more costly than the brown malt which was the basis of the extremely popular porter.

Ironically the very popularity of porter led to its downfall and to the introduction and acceptance of pale beers. The characteristic subacid flavor (an underlying, subtle acidity) of the heavily hopped porter could be achieved only by long maturation in huge wooden vats. Only the commercial brewers could produce it economically in the volume required by the rapidly growing numbers of thirsty city-dwellers. As a result, the late 18th century saw a phenomenal growth in both the number

7

and size of brewing companies, and a concomitant decrease in pub- and homebrewing.

Because of their growth and profitability, the porter brewers were able to invest money in developing and adopting new technologies. Many advances, such as the use of steam power, were made during this period, for Britain's Industrial Revolution was in full stride. The most important development, as far as the story of pale ale is concerned, was the introduction of the thermometer and the hydrometer to the brewing process.

These instruments gave the brewer much better control over the mashing stage and allowed him, for the first time, to determine what he was getting out of his malt. One result of this was the realization that pale malts were not more expensive than brown malts, in terms of actual extract per unit cost. This led to a fairly rapid adoption of the modern approach, where pale malt is used as the extract base, with stronger flavors and darker colors being obtained by the addition of relatively small amounts of highly roasted malts. It would take only a small step from there to the ready acceptance of beers brewed only from pale malt.

THE FIRST INDIA PALE ALE

In the last century, Charles Stuart Calverley wrote an interesting piece of blank verse:

Oh Beer! O Hodgson, Guinness, Allsop, Bass!
Names that should be on every infant's tongue!

It is interesting because it has an odd man out, which isn't Guinness, even though the others are all pale ale brewers. It's Hodgson, the least well-known name of the quartet, because unlike the others, it has not survived as a modern brewing company.

Hodgson is odd man out for two reasons. First, he was a London brewer, and London was noted for its dark, not its pale beers. Second, he was noted as a pale ale brewer in the latter half of the 18th century, long before any other individual brewer on record. In fact, Hodgson initiated and, until about 1820, monopolized the export of beer to India.

So, although he may have called it simply "India Ale," Hodgson was the originator of IPA. What's more, this really means that IPA was defined before pale ale itself was truly established. Which is to say that the subcategory was actually the precursor of the modern style! This is why, as we shall see later, the decision as to whether a particular beer is a pale ale, bitter, or IPA may have to be made on purely arbitrary grounds instead of for historical reasons.

If Hodgson's IPA was the original, then it would be instructive to see what it was really like. Of course, we shall never know how it tasted, but there are some clues which might help us get a feel for what sort of beer it was.

The first of these is strength. Porters, stouts and other styles of beer around 1800 were very strong. Original gravities of 1.070 to 1.100 (17 to 26 °P) were the norm and IPA, as a beer designed to survive months of rough traveling in a very hot climate, would have been brewed to this kind of strength. It would have been very well-attenuated and high in alcohol by the time it was drunk.

It also would have been heavily hopped, because the preservative value of hops was considered very important in those days. Also, the high level of hop bitterness would have helped to hide any flavor defects which developed during the beer's long journey. We cannot tell just how bitter this beer really was, because we do not know which hops were used. Goldings, which later became the favored hop for pale ales, were introduced around 1780, but we do not know how available they were. Nor do we know what kind of alpha-acid content hops had in those days, although we can guess it was probably lower than that of modern hops. But this is pure speculation. This was a time when even the role of yeast and the nature of fermentation were not understood. The complexities of hop chemistry were unimaginable.

Nevertheless, a group of dedicated English homebrewers, the Durden Park Beer Circle, has reconstructed a recipe for Original India Pale Ale. It uses only pale malt, has an OG of 1.070 (17 °P) and uses 2.1 ounces of Goldings per gallon. Assuming 5 percent alpha acid for the hops, this amounts to 52.5 HBU per five gallons (150 to 200 IBU)! I haven't tried to brew this beer yet, but that's an extremely high bittering rate, although alpha-acid utilization is probably poorer than at more normal hopping levels.

One other important point should be made about Hodgson's IPA. Bottles were not widely used in commercial brewing at that time, so it would have been a draught beer, shipped in wooden casks. As such, it probably had a subacid flavor from the action of secondary yeasts and species such as Brettanomyces. In addition, it probably would have been fairly low in carbon dioxide content by the time the cask was broached.

COMPETITION, PALE ALE, AND BOTTLES

Hodgson's early domination of the Indian beer trade was partly a matter of transport. It was much easier and cheaper to move bulk beer around the country by water

Wooden casks in cellar.

than by road. For brewers in the central part of England, such as Burton, the Trent Navigation Canal offered a cheap, direct route to the great North Sea port of Hull, and thence to Northern Europe.

The Burton brewers developed a lucrative export market with Russia and the Baltic countries. In the early 1800s they lost this market, partly because of the Napoleonic Blockade and partly because the Russians imposed prohibitive tariffs on beer imports. At the same time, demand for beer was growing in India and Hodgson himself had to expand his brewery in 1821.

The Burton brewers quite naturally turned to India to replace their lost Russian trade. Allsopp developed a pale ale in 1822, soon to be followed by Bass, Ratcliff and a few others. Certain London brewers, such as Charrington, also jumped on the bandwagon as beer and porter exports virtually doubled from 1830 to 1840.

11

As an export beer, of course, IPA was not sold in Britain at first. Legend has it that one India-bound ship was wrecked in the Irish Sea. Supposedly, part of its cargo of Bass IPA was salvaged and auctioned off in Liverpool. The English drinkers who sampled it were so impressed that they demanded more, which the brewers did their best to supply.

That is probably apocryphal. What is more likely is that public tastes were changing in England. The Burton brewers in particular, having solved the problem of producing a high-quality pale ale for export, realized that they could make a similar beer for home consumption and started to offer it for sale in their normal trading areas. Such beers would not need to be quite so strong and heavily hopped as IPA, but were otherwise very much in the same style.

Other factors came into play also. As the Industrial Revolution burgeoned, the bigger cities grew rapidly in population, becoming major markets themselves. With the rapid growth of both the road and rail networks, it became much easier for the Burton brewers to transport their wares to places like London. Pale beers began to seriously compete with porter.

The Burton brewers prospered as a result of these changes. By 1853 Bass had built a second brewery at Burton and a third was erected only 10 years later. As pale ale consumption rapidly grew, it became apparent that Burton was brewing the finest pale ales, partly because of the high mineral content of its brewing water. Between 1850 and 1875 several big London brewers opened up breweries in Burton. These included some still-famous names, such as Charrington's (now merged with Bass), Ind Coope (which later took over Allsopp and is now a part of the Allied empire), Truman's and Mann & Crossman (both absorbed into the Grand Metropolitan conglomerate, along with Watney's).

We must consider one other factor which promoted the growth of pale ale drinking and also had an effect on our modern perception of what the style should be. The first reference to bottled beers being shipped to India was in 1830, and even then it was a minor item compared to the amount of draught beer shipped. Bottled beer had been known in England since the 17th century, but although bottles were often exported to America they were not widely used in England, where draught beer remained a firm favorite.

What is more, up until about 1840 glass drinking vessels were not common in England or in most other countries. Pilsener was invented about this time, and it was the first truly pale beer the world had known. It is no coincidence that Bohemia soon became a major glass-manufacturing area and that industrially produced glass rapidly displaced pewter and stoneware drinking vessels.

In Britain there had been a heavy tax on glass for many years. This was removed in 1845, just as mass-production techniques for bottles and glasses were being developed. The introduction of glass containers had a profound effect on the brewing industry. Previously most drinkers had worried only about the taste of their beer; now they could see it as well.

Once consumers were able to look at what they were drinking the trend in favor of pale beers gathered speed. They also began to demand that their beers should be clear, not murky. Accordingly, the technique of fining draught beer with isinglass became more widespread in England. It is still practiced there today in the production of traditional cask beer. The demand for brilliantly clear beer helped promote the use of bottles, a trend also

Historical version of the trademark Bass label.

accelerated later in the 19th century by the application of several scientific discoveries to the brewing process. These were pasteurization, refrigeration, filtration and artificial carbonation. Artificial carbonation and filtration enabled pub owners to bypass the conditioning period of real ale, which takes a great deal of care. Both pasteurization and refrigeration allowed the bottled beer to keep longer. And while beer in wooden casks could be filtered and refrigerated, pasteurization and artificial carbonation in a wooden container are simply not feasible. These techniques were later applied to draught beers, almost resulting in the disappearance of cask-conditioned beers in recent times.

The first trademark in Britain was taken out in 1890 by Bass and was a bottle label for pale ale. Later it was immortalized by Manet in his earlier portrait of the wistful girl behind the bar of the Folies Bergere. At that stage, it would have been a bottle-conditioned beer and a direct precursor of today's Worthington White Shield, the only naturally conditioned bottled pale ale left in Britain. Worthington, for the record, was a Burton brewer who had been taken over by Bass back in the 18th century.

Michael Jackson, in his *New World Guide to Beer*, shows two Bass bottles of about 1930 vintage which bear the Bass Pale Ale trademark label. These bottles also carry a second label, presumably applied by the London bottler and inscribed "East India Pale Ale." Apparently even those in the trade were not clear about the difference between pale ale and IPA at this late stage!

Although bottled beers became more common, especially in the 20th century, they never came close to dominating the English market. At its maximum, bottled beer made up only 30 percent of total English consumption; it is currently around 20 percent and still falling. One important reason for this is the English predilection for drinking in the pub, rather than at home or elsewhere.

Another reason is the very big difference in taste between draught and bottled versions of the same beer. Pale ale grists are mashed by the single-temperature infusion process, often at temperatures no higher than 150 degrees F (65.5 degrees C), so that the wort is relatively low in unfermentable dextrins. Fermentation is carried out at fairly high temperatures—60 to 65 degrees F (16 to 18 degrees C)—and is often followed by warm conditioning at around 55 degrees F (13 degrees C) for up to one month. Draught beers then undergo a final conditioning in the pub cellar during which excess carbon dioxide is allowed to escape. The resulting beer is well-attenuated, having a dry, rather than a malty flavor, and is low in carbonation (about one volume). Both these factors allow hop bitterness to dominate the beer's palate.

When the same beer is bottled, it is usually carbonated to about two volumes. Because of the beer's dryness, this gives it a prickly bite which masks the hop flavor, thus spoiling its most important characteristic. While some of the finest examples of the genre can carry high carbonation, most are reduced to blandness and apparent mediocrity by this procedure. This was an important campaigning point for the members of CAMRA, who complained about the "fizzy" nature of the highly carbonated keg beers with which the big brewers tried to replace cask-conditioned ales.

But whether bottled or cask, pale beers gained ground over their darker rivals throughout the 19th century. Porter in particular lost out badly, and disappeared entirely in the twentieth century. Even its derivative, mild ale, has had a difficult time in recent years, losing sales almost everywhere and being entirely replaced by pale beers in some parts of England.

Pale ale is actually amber in color. It gets its name only because it is pale in comparison to dark beers. Porters and stouts were the foundation on which the modern British brewery industry was built, and they enjoyed immense popularity for well over a hundred years. As a result, they set the standards against which other beers were judged.

There is a good reason why pale ale is not really pale. British barley is of the two-row variety, which is relatively low in nitrogen. The malting process is intensive, and kilning temperatures are high, so that pale ale malt is highly modified, low in enzymes, and fairly highly colored. This means it can be mashed by the single-temperature infusion technique, which produces beers with a reddish or copper color, rather than the yellow color obtained from pale lager malts.

That was certainly the case in the last century. However, modern malting techniques have improved so much that pale ale malts can now be produced to make beers with a relatively pale, golden-yellow color. Most brewers still aim for the classical red-copper tint, which nowadays is achieved by adding a small proportion of highly roasted crystal malt to the mash.

BITTER AND MODERN TIMES

Bitter is considered to be a subcategory of pale ale. Yet if we take the view that pale ale is primarily a bottled beer, then bitter is now the more important of the two, in terms of the volume drunk in England. With the exception of lager, bitter is undoubtedly the most popular British beer today.

Despite its popularity, the origin and history of bitter are even more obscure than those of pale ale. Michael Jackson states that its acceptance as a formal style is relatively recent, and suggests that the name "bitter" may not have been fully established even as late as the 1940s. With some trepidation, I have to disagree with him for once. There are several references to bitter ales in the last century. As far back as 1857, one writer discusses pale ale and India pale ale under the generic title of "Bitter Ales."

An 1884 brewer's price list quotes a "Light Bitter Ale." There are no descriptive details, but the price suggests it was brewed to a significantly lower gravity than the same brewer's pale ale. On the other hand, in 1910 another brewer lists several pale ales and even a "Light Ale." Yet there is no mention of a bitter in a quite comprehensive assortment of ales, stouts and porters.

In 1881 a Professor Graham published what might be regarded as a landmark paper in a still extant scientific journal. It was entitled "On Lager Beer" and was an attempt to persuade British brewers to move away from heavily hopped, strong, top-fermented beers, to lighter, less bitter lagers. Graham's listeners were probably highly skeptical of his message, but from our perspective he had a remarkably clear view of the future!

Graham quotes the original gravities of both Burton pale (1.062 or 15 °P) and Burton bitter (1.064 or 15.7 °P), as well as of "AK bitter" (1.045 or 11 °P) and Scotch bitter (1.057 or 14 °P). The latter is as well-attenuated as the other bitters, although Scotch ales are generally considered to have a much sweeter finish than their English counterparts. What is more, both the Burton and AK bitters were brewed at lower gravities than their corresponding mild ales (1.080 or 19.4 °P for the Burton, and 1.055 or 13.6 °P to 1.074 or 18 °P for the AK milds)!

Unfortunately for us, Graham does not elaborate on the difference between Burton pale and bitter. He does point out that they were highly attenuated, with finishing gravities as low as one-quarter to one-fifth of the original gravity. These were high-alcohol beers, at 6.7 percent v/v. (volume of alcohol per volume of solution) or 5.4 percent w/v. (weight of alcohol per volume of solution), and 6.8 percent v/v. or 5.4 percent w/v., respectively.

Graham's comments on hop rates are interesting. He quotes the addition of 16 pounds of copper hops (hops added to the "copper," or boiling kettle) and two pounds of dry hops to five English barrels of bitter ale at an original gravity of 1.045 (implying that the latter is a fairly standard figure for bitter ales). That works out to six ounces per five U.S. gallons in the copper, and about three-quarters ounces for dry-hopping. Again, we have no numbers on the alpha-acid values of these hops. By that time it is a good guess that they were Goldings, which we can assume might have contained 5 percent alpha acid. That amounts to 30 HBU per five gallons (about 110 IBU), which is still very high by modern standards.

One of the difficulties of tracing the origin of bitter is that this may have been a colloquialism for any pale beer. Or, since it is descriptive of the beer's flavor, it may simply have been applied to any pale beer which was not considered to be deserving of the title "Pale Ale." That could be because a particular brewer offered both a pale ale and a lower-gravity bitter. Or it could have been that any pale beer brewed outside of Burton would not be called pale ale, almost as though this designation was an appellation controlée.

Perhaps that is a little fanciful. Yet, although Burton brewers did not originate the style, they certainly did brew the best pale ales, and their ability to do so was a big factor in its rapid growth in popularity. Surely other brewers tried to emulate these brews in their own locality. They would have used locally available raw materials and probably had some difficulty in matching Burton products.

Even at this stage many of the smaller brewers outside of the great brewing centers like Burton and London had only a fairly rudimentary knowledge of and control over the brewing process. Often they did their own malting, probably from barley of very variable quality, so that their pale malt itself was inferior to that used by the more advanced big brewers in Burton.

However, thanks largely to Pasteur's work, the role of yeast in brewing was now understood and progress was being made in developing large-scale fermentation systems. This was crucial to pale ale production because of the need for full attenuation of the beer. Most brewers were still using traditional, round vessels with a simple skimming system to handle yeast removal. For pale ale production such a setup may not have been ideally suited to the yeast strains used by individual brewers.

The Burton brewers, on the other hand, had developed a unique approach to fermentation with their famous Burton Union System. It must be said that it is not clear whether the system was developed to suit the yeast or whether the yeast adapted itself to the system.

Slate tanks of the Yorkshire Stone Square system.

Whichever the case, the result was that a clear finished beer could be readily produced with a very powdery yeast. Such yeasts do not settle easily. Because they stay in suspension longer than more flocculent yeasts, they give higher attenuations than the latter—perfect for a pale ale.

Yorkshire brewers in another important pale ale brewing center, Tadcaster, had a different type of yeast and developed their own technique for handling it. This was the Yorkshire Stone Square System. It is a circulating system like the Burton Unions, but with a very different purpose. Circulation in the Unions is designed to achieve good separation of a poor-settling yeast from the beer. The Yorkshire brewers had a highly flocculent yeast which would rapidly settle out, giving poor attenuation in traditional "rounds." So the Stone Square circulation system was designed to continually rouse the fermenting wort, keeping the yeast in suspension until full attenuation had been achieved. A side effect of using such yeasts is that the beer may have high levels of diacetyl; the resulting "butterscotch" flavor is often an accepted characteristic of beers brewed in this way. Incidentally, in the British homebrewing revival of the 1960s and 70s, such rousing was mistakenly assumed to be essential for all yeasts and recipes often recommended rousing the wort twice daily. Not only is this usually unnecessary, it is also an excellent way of starting bacterial infections!

One factor above all limited the country brewers' attempts to emulate their big brothers in Burton. That, of course, was the quality of their brewing water. It was no accident that the best porter was produced in London and the best pale ales in Burton, Tadcaster, Alton, Dorchester and so on. As we now know, those areas had the right mineral content to give the correct mashing pH and hence optimum extraction from the malt.

Burton water in particular had very high levels of calcium (~200 to 300 ppm), magnesium (50 to 60 ppm), and sulphate ions (600 to 800 ppm). These ions are not only beneficial to the brewing process, but also influence beer flavor. Sulfate, especially, makes the beer appear to be drier, enhancing the high hop bitterness typical of pale ales.

In the late 19th century, the beneficial aspects of certain types of water were well-known to brewers. But they had no way of changing an unsuitable water. Techniques of softening water and treatment with salts such as gypsum ("Burtonisation") had not been developed. Therefore, they had to go with what they had, with the result that their attempts at pale ale may have been darker in color and with a coarser hop flavor than the clean, sharp bitterness of a top-quality pale. Rather than call such beers pale ales, the brewers may have felt it was easier

21

to ward off criticism by promoting them as the separate style "Bitter Ale."

Whatever the precise origin of its name, bitter is now well-established in Britain. As the move away from dark beers accelerated in this century, especially after the Second World War, it was bitter rather than pale ale that replaced porter and has almost ousted mild ale. This is partly because there was an accompanying trend to reduce the original gravities of beers in general. The average original gravity for all English beers is now under 1.040 (10 °P), whereas 100 years ago it was 1.055 (13.6 °P).

Traditional, cask-conditioned beer was also on its way to extinction until CAMRA came along in the 1970s. It is not an easy product to handle, since controlling the secondary fermentation in the pub cellar requires a good deal of skill from the publican. Further, once it is opened for serving, air enters the cask, so the beer must be consumed rapidly or it will spoil.

Brewers tried to overcome these problems by chilling, filtering, and pasteurizing the beer, then artificially carbonating and dispensing from a keg with carbon-dioxide pressure. At its best such beer is overgassed. More often it has also been deliberately brewed blander, sweeter and less hoppy than a true bitter. This is certainly true of some of the big name beers such as Bass, Watney's, and Whitbread, which are sold as "draught" in the United States.

Although CAMRA definitely reversed the keg beer trend back towards real ale, keg beer is still very much with us and the future of cask-conditioned beer in doubt. It is difficult for the homebrewer to make and even more difficult for the microbrewer to sell in the United States. But if you want to brew pale ales and bitters at their best then you must come as close to the original, more natural way of dispensing them as possible.

ADJUNCTS—USE OR ABUSE?

England never had a Reinheitsgebot purity law, but before 1800 the Inland Revenue did not permit brewers to use anything other than malt and hops. A special order allowed the use of sugar for the years of 1800, 1812 and 1813, and in 1847 all restrictions on sugar in brewing were removed. It still didn't become widely used in Britain, for it was taxed as heavily as malt.

Then, in 1880, Prime Minister of England Sir William Gladstone introduced his so-called "Free Mash Tun Act." This removed all taxes on raw materials and based beer duty solely on wort original gravity. At the time it may have seemed a very logical approach, but it had three far-reaching consequences:

(1) The Act taxed homebrewers at virtually the same rate as the commercial companies. Already on the wane, homebrewing soon died out almost completely, only reviving when the provisions of the Act were repealed in 1963.

(2) The standard tax rate was based on an OG of 1.057 (14 °P), the average for the time. Stronger beers paid more, weaker ones paid less. As tax rates increased in later years, stronger beers were disproportionately penalized and average gravities inevitably declined.

(3) After the Act, the Inland Revenue was concerned only with the wort. They no longer cared what kind of raw materials the brewers used—hence the name of the Act. This meant that malt substitutes could now be added to the brew.

Adjuncts did not become popular overnight, but their use in British brewing is now the norm except perhaps by some of the new micros. A typical modern

British grist contains about 10 to 15 percent non-malt cereal, 5 to 10 percent sugar, and 80 percent pale and roast malts.

Both the cereal and sugar are supposedly "nitrogen diluents," reducing the amount of nitrogenous material in the beer and lowering the risk of chill-haze formation. The sugar, often added as invert sugar (a glucose:fructose mixture), is also said to make for a drier beer since it is totally fermentable. Certain cereals may also improve beer head retention.

The most common cereal is flaked maize (corn), but wheat flour is popular, too. Modern wet-milling technology permits the use of a good proportion of unmalted barley, especially if manufactured enzymes are added. Most of the better brewers avoid this adjunct, especially in pale ale brewing.

Whatever the brewers say, I believe their real reason for using adjuncts is that they are cheaper than malt. It is revealing that they use a misleading name for what are actually *malt substitutes*. In my view, the permutations available from the use of pale and roasted malts, together with sound brewing and serving techniques, mean that adjuncts are unnecessary.

On the other hand, I have to admit that some of my favorite English beers, world classics by any standard, are brewed with a proportion of adjuncts. I could say, "How much better still would they be if they were malt-only beers?" but that may be nit-picking. It comes down to opinion, so we shall deal with adjunct usage in the chapters on brewing and recipes and you can decide where you stand on this issue yourself, preferably after some trial brews!

2

Character Profile of Pale Ale

The style and its subcategories can be defined with some fairly precise analytical numbers and flavor descriptions. But it should be clear from the last chapter that there is a considerable overlap between pale ale, India pale ale, and bitter ale. You might think that the confusion of styles could be clarified by looking at the versions of these beers sold in England today. Surely the brewers know their own beers, and will have labeled them properly?

Not a chance! They are even more confused than we are! A survey of all the traditional draught beers offered by English brewers, under the names pale ale, IPA, and bitter, reveals that there is a total of 461 such beers. Only 11 of these are called pale ale, with a mere five earning the IPA designation, the remainder being designated as bitter.

Seven of those pale ales and two of the IPAs have original gravities below 1.035 (8.7 °P), despite the fact that history says the latter should be the strongest of the three. In contrast, there are no less than 30 bitters in the range 1.050 to 1.060 (12 to 15 °P). Of course, a number of those bitters when bottled would be called pale ale, since many brewers consider the term refers only to bottled beer, which was not included in the survey. However, there are even a few pitfalls in that approach. Young's of London, who brewed the first beer I ever drank, brew a bottled ale of note. It has an OG of 1.062 (15 °P) and a high bitterness (50 to 55 IBU) which ought to put it squarely in the IPA category. In fact, it is labelled Special Export Bitter!

Even Michael Jackson finds it difficult to separate pale ale and bitter, suggesting that in some cases the difference between them is purely a matter of semantics. He takes the approach that bitter is the "ordinary" brew under that designation, whereas pale ale is the premium bitter, usually, but not always, in the bottled form. I have to agree with him, and I think it is fair to say that this view is a pretty good synthesis of the unwritten definitions assigned to these beers by English drinkers.

However, defining what constitutes a "Premium Bitter" is no simple matter. Some brewers do not have one, whilst others have no "Ordinary Bitter." Some brewers' weakest beers match the premiums offered by other brewers. I am therefore going to make the distinction between bitter, pale ale and IPA largely on the grounds of original gravity, tempered by our historical knowledge of the characteristics of each style.

Bitter will be considered as having OG 1.035 to 1.045 (8.7 to 11 °P), and pale ale 1.045 to 1.055 (11 to 13.5 °P). IPA will be at the top end of the pale ale specification, 1.050 to 1.055 (12.3 to 13.5 °P), with a higher hop bitterness than pale ale.

Bear in mind that there are wide variations in the flavors of pale ales and bitters brewed in England, many of them regional. Levels of sweetness, color, hop bitterness, hop aroma, carbonation and even dispensing techniques vary widely. The profiles that follow are necessarily restrictive, so you should regard them as being merely guidelines. The recipes and brewing information in this book can ultimately form a basis for the development of your own version of the style. Remember, pale ale is difficult to define because it is a living style; like a language, it changes all the time.

Historical pale ale, bitter and India pale ale labels.

PROFILES

- Pale Ale -

Original Specific Gravity: 1.045–1.055 (11–13.5 °P)
Apparent Final Gravity: 1.009–1.013 (2.2–3.3 °P)
Apparent Degree of Attenuation: 75–80%
Real Degree of Attenuation: 55–65%
Reducing Sugars (as maltose): 1–2%
Acidity (as lactic acid): 0.2%
pH: 3.9–4.2
Bitterness: 7–13 HBU per 5 gallons; 25–45 IBU
Color: 8–14 °L
Alcohol: 3.8–4.4 w/v.; 4.8–5.5 v/v.

A few points of explanation are necessary here. I have deliberately omitted CO_2 levels from the profile because it depends on whether the beer is to be draught or bottled. Cask-conditioned draught pale ales have a low carbonation level: 0.75 to 1.0 volumes. The lesser quality keg versions are more gassy, at 1.3 to 2.0 volumes, while bottled pale ale should be 1.5 to 2.0 volumes. Higher levels are *totally inappropriate to the style* since the acidic, prickly effect of excessive amounts of gas will mask the essential, bitter hop flavor.

Final gravity should be about one-quarter OG, although lower levels are well-suited to the style. Higher finishing gravities are acceptable, but may require operating at the top end of the bittering range. The beer should be highly attenuated, and if the finishing gravity is higher than indicated it should be due only to a high dextrin level and not to the presence of unfermented sugars. Color can vary from the range indicated, particularly if

28

the beer is to be regarded as a draught premium bitter. If it is intended to be a classic bottled pale ale such as, say, Worthington White Shield, then the low end of the range given is appropriate.

Finally, bitterness. If it is not already clear to you, let me emphasize again that the outstanding characteristic of this beer is a definite, even pronounced hop bitterness. If your beer doesn't have this it isn't pale ale, no matter how good it tastes! Lower bittering levels than those indicated are simply unacceptable for this style.

- Aroma and Flavor of Pale Ale -

Let's take flavor first. Pale ale should have a clean, malty fullness on the front of the palate, with fruity, estery overtones, followed by a long, lingering hop bitterness on the back of the palate. The bitterness should be clean, with no astringency, and there should be no solventlike character in the fruitiness, nor any lingering sweetness to hide the hop flavor. If the beer is dry- or late-hopped, it will also have an aromatic hop character, preferably of a floral or lightly resinous nature. It is also acceptable, but not essential, to have a butterscotch flavor due to the presence of diacetyl.

The aroma of draught pale ale may be difficult to detect because of the low carbonation level. Therefore, aroma is a more important characteristic in the bottled version. Even then it may be fairly delicate, with only a faint, slightly grainy, malty note underneath a light fruitiness. If aroma hops have been used, then a floral, spicy or grassy odor may dominate. If the beer is high in diacetyl, then it may also have a quite distinct buttery aroma.

From the above you will see that the use of aroma hops is optional. Some brewers use them, some do not; of

29

those who do, some late-hop, some dry-hop in the cask, one English brewer dry-hops in the fermenter. There are no hard and fast rules as to which aroma hop variety should be used, either. East Kent Goldings are the traditional pale ale hop for bittering and for dry-hopping in the cask. As an aroma hop, the Golding gives the beer a nicely delicate floral/grassy character without dominating other flavor notes. However, other aroma hops are used by English brewers, notably Saaz, Hallertauer and Styrian Goldings, whilst Cascades have been used in some excellent American pale ales.

~ India Pale Ale ~

Original Specific Gravity: 1.050–1.055 (12.3–13.5 °P)
Apparent Final Gravity: 1.011–1.014 (2.8–3.5 °P)
Apparent Degree of Attenuation: 72–78%
Real Degree of Attenuation: 53–65%
Reducing Sugars (as maltose): 1–2%
Acidity (as lactic acid): 0.2%
pH: 3.9–4.2
Bitterness: 11–15 HBU per 5 gallons; 40–55 IBU
Color: 8–14 °L
Alcohol: 4.1–4.5 w/v.; 5.1–5.6 v/v.

Most of the comments on pale ale are also pertinent here. The exceptions are that this beer is more bitter and can therefore carry a slightly higher final gravity. So long as this is from a higher dextrin level there should still be virtually no unfermented sugars. The higher bitterness also means that this beer can withstand carbonation better than most pale ales, so that it loses little on bottling.

I have indicated that the color level is the same as for pale ale, but that is not strictly true. IPA, especially in its bottled form, should be as pale in color as possible. Its slightly higher gravity will make that difficult in an all-malt brew, unless the addition of roasted (i.e. crystal) malt is kept to a minimum.

- Aroma and Flavor of India Pale Ale -

Most of the comments under pale ale apply here. Because this brew is a little higher in alcohol, the fruity, estery aroma may be a little more pronounced. IPA should also have a more malty nose than pale ale. Again, the use of aroma hops is optional but does add much to the beer's character, especially when achieved by dry hopping with Goldings. The buttery odor of diacetyl is perhaps undesirable in IPA.

In flavor, as in aroma, the fruity and malty characters of this brew are a little more apparent than they are in pale ale. The dominant flavor is an almost overpowering hop bitterness. IPA is the most bitter beer of the major styles, and as such may require some getting used to on the part of those accustomed to less hoppy brews. It is absolutely essential that there be no harshness or astringency in this bitterness, so the hops used must be as fresh as possible.

An impressive and highly individualistic U.S. example of this beer is (was?) Ballantine India Pale Ale. Supposedly made from an authentic 19th century English recipe, brewed to a high gravity, heavily dry-hopped and aged in oak casks, this beer has a very intense, complex aromatic character (or did have until the last few years or so). Some of this character, as with a good white wine, came from the oak; homebrewers, under the impression that this flavor was essential to the style, have tried to reproduce it by adding oak chips to their beer.

In fact, "oakiness" is not a characteristic of English

Top-fermented beer in high kraeusen at Young's Brewery.

IPA, although the beer was and sometimes still is aged in wood. You see, English oak is very different from its American cousin, and imparts little or no flavor to beer stored in casks made from it. Indeed, I remember a conversation with one of Britain's few remaining brewers' coopers, in which he said they would never use American oak, "because it would spoil the beer's flavor!"

- Bitter Ale -

Original Specific Gravity: 1.035–1.045 (8.7–11.0 °P)
Apparent Final Gravity: 1.008–1.011 (2.0–2.8 °P)
Apparent Degree of Attenuation: 70–80%
Real Degree of Attenuation: 53–65%
Reducing Sugars (as maltose): 1–2.5%
Acidity (as lactic acid): 0.2%
pH: 3.9–4.2
Bitterness: 5–9 HBU per 5 gallons; 20–35 IBU

Color: 8–20 °L
Alcohol: 2.9–3.5% w/v.; 3.6–4.5% v/v.
Carbon dioxide: 0.75%; 1 volume

The first point to note is that I have given the carbonation level in the profile. That is because this is *unequivocally* a draught beer. Like pale ale, it is still highly attenuated, but being of a lower original gravity it has less body, so that it is essential not to overcarbonate and hide its hop bitterness.

The color range is wider than for pale ale. This simply reflects current practice, for bitter ranges in color from almost golden, through copper, to a ruby tinge. In short, higher levels of crystal malt can be used to make this beer than would be the case with pale ale.

Some examples of bitter are a little more bitter than most pale ales. That is because there is less malt body in a bitter, so there is little to balance the hop bitterness. Do not overdo this, as high residual sugar is definitely inappropriate to the style.

- Aroma and Flavor of Bitter -

If aroma hops are used, which is optional for the style, this should come through first. Otherwise, because of the lower gravity both malty and estery notes are muted in this beer. The buttery odor of diacetyl is still acceptable, but since there is little else to offset it, it can be easily overdone.

This beer should have a definite, but not strong, fruity flavor. It may be malty, but this is often minimal. It may also have a resiny, aromatic hop flavor. The best examples are dry-hopped, but the use of aroma hops is

33

optional. The dominating flavor of this beer is hop bitterness—it isn't called bitter for nothing. Because of low original gravity, many bitters are actually hoppier in flavor than their stronger "premium" counterparts.

It is worth remembering that most bitters are "session" beers. That is, they are designed to be interesting in flavor, yet relatively low in alcohol. That way they can be enjoyed throughout a whole evening's pleasant conversation and companionship in the pub without overwhelming the drinker.

3

How Pale Ale is Brewed

INGREDIENTS

- Malt -

Pale Malt. This is the workhorse for pale ale. It is the main source of fermentable material and provides much of the color. For the finest pale ales and IPAs it may be the only source of color and fermentables, as well as much of the non-hop flavor. It is therefore essential to use pale malt of the highest quality, meaning one that is designed for pale ale production.

You will not be surprised to hear that this means it must be a British pale malt. Yes, British, not just English, for Scotland grows some of the finest malting barley and therefore produces very high quality pale malt. Some of this Scottish malt, of course, goes to make that other famous product!

British pale malt is made from two-row barley, whereas most American pale malt comes from six-row varieties. British pale malt is low in nitrogen and well-modified, which means that the germination of the barley grain has been allowed to go a little further than is the case with pale lager malts. These factors mean that pale ale malt, as I shall call it from now on, is relatively low in protein. A low-temperature proteolytic step prior to saccharification is not required in mashing well-modified malts.

Pale ale malts are kilned at fairly high temperatures, up to about 200 degrees F (95 degrees C) in the final stages. This gives it a darker color than pale lager malt, which is why most pale ales are copper-colored rather than golden. The higher kilning, as well as certain other factors, means that pale malts have a low enzyme content.

The last statement needs a little explaining. The enzyme content is still very high in comparison to, say, roasted malts such as crystal or chocolate. I use the term low only in respect to other pale malts; in particular, it is much lower than the enzyme content of pale malt prepared from American six-row barleys. These latter have an excess of starch-degrading enzymes, so they can convert not only their own starch, but also that of a considerable quantity of starch adjuncts. This is why U.S. brewers can add 50 percent or more of non-malt adjuncts such as rice and corn to their mash.

Pale ale malt, on the other hand, cannot handle anywhere near this level of adjuncts. It has sufficient enzyme content to degrade its own starch to dextrins, plus fermentable sugars, with a little to spare. This is why English brewers who use starch-based adjuncts generally limit them to about 10 to 15 percent of the grist.

Because it is well-modified, pale ale malt is mashed by the traditional single-step infusion method at around 150 degrees F (65.5 degrees C). The main aim of mashing is simply conversion of starch and extraction of fermentables. The starch is not locked in a protein matrix and is easily exposed to enzyme action. All you need to do is to crack the grain so that the mash water can get at the starch. It is not at all necessary to grind this malt to get high levels of extract, as is often the case with pale lager malts.

It is fairly easy to crack pale ale malt grains and leave the husks intact but separate from the starchy kernel. The unbroken husks ensure that the grain bed is nicely permeable so that it does not clog, or "set," during wort runoff and sparging. This is why British commercial brewers perform these operations in the mash tun. It is not necessary to have a lauter tun, as in lager brewing. The homebrewer does not need a separate lauter tun either, so long as his mash tun is designed for bottom run-off.

A typical analysis for pale ale malt is as follows:

Moisture: 1.5–3.0%
Nitrogen: 1.5–1.6%
Total Soluble Nitrogen: 0.5–0.6%
Diastatic Power: 35–45 °Lintner
Color: 2.5–3 °L
Extract: 78–80%; 34–36 °specific gravity per pound per gallon

The extract information needs a little explaining. The percentage figure is that obtained with a standard American Society of Brewing Chemists test. Homebrew suppliers may have or may be able to get the batch analysis for you. However, the second number is more useful to us. It means that one pound of malt will produce one gallon of wort with OG 1.034 to 1.036 (8.4 to 8.9 °P). This is actually the maximum you can expect to achieve. In practice, you will probably get a lower figure, 30 to 31 degrees specific gravity per pound per gallon being as much as most homebrewers can expect.

37

British pale ale malt is now widely available in the United States and the quality is excellent. Since it is perfect for the style there is no reason to use anything else. Canadian and U.S. pale malts from two- and six-row barleys can be used if you really want to experiment, but they are generally too light in flavor to make a good pale ale. Although they can be mashed by single-stage infusion, their high nitrogen levels (about 2 percent) will likely cause haze problems. A low-temperature proteolysis stage is usually required. A discussion of such procedures is beyond the scope of this book, since they are most suited to lager-brewing.

Crystal Malt. This is normally the only roasted malt that is used in pale ale brewing. It adds a little color, intensifying the copper hue, and provides a little extra body and mouth feel to balance the beer's hoppiness. Typically it is added at the rate of about 5 percent of the total grist. That means about four ounces for a beer of OG 1.048 (12 °P). Larger proportions can be used, but may give the beer an undesirably coarse flavor if overdone.

Naturally, British crystal malt should be used for pale ale. It is made by taking fully modified green malt and heating, or "stewing," it at around 160 degrees F (71 degrees C) with virtually no ventilation, so that little moisture evaporation occurs. Under these conditions the starch is degraded to sugars, which are caramelized as the kilning temperature is increased to around 240 degrees F (116 degrees C). If you examine a grain of this malt you will see that the kernel is brown and glassy compared to the white, floury nature of a pale malt kernel.

There are no enzymes to speak of left in crystal malt, and all its desirable qualities are easily extractable by leaching with hot water. It can therefore be used in a malt extract brew with no complication of procedures. In an all-grain brew it is simply ground with the pale malt and extracted in the mash itself.

A typical analysis for a British crystal malt is given below:

Moisture: 3–4%
Color: 30–100 °L
Extract: 60–65%; 25–28 °specific gravity per pound per gallon

For most British crystal malt available in the United States you can base your color calculations on 60 °L. With only a small proportion of crystal malt being used in this type of beer, its contribution to the original gravity of extract brewing can be ignored in many cases.

Since it is widely available in the United States and is the traditional roasted malt used in pale ale brewing, British crystal malt is the first choice if you want to duplicate an authentic British pale ale. However, it need not be the only choice. A number of suppliers are now offering a whole range of crystal malts, usually of American origin. These come in a variety of colors. They may simply have descriptive names, such as "light," "amber," or "dark," but most of the suppliers who offer them will actually give their color analyses also. I have a catalogue which lists five types, at 20 °L, 40 °L, 60 °L, 80 °L, and 90 °L. The lowest number will be more of a golden color, and they become more red-brown as the Lovibond number increases.

These are all genuine crystal malts, so there is no reason why they cannot be used in making a good version of your own pale ale. Since the intensity of caramelization increases with color, they offer the opportunity to vary both flavor and color of the brew. If you are trying to brew a pale, golden bitter such as Boddington's Bitter from

Manchester or Theakston's Best Bitter from Yorkshire, then a light crystal malt can be used to give the brew good mouth feel with little darkening of the pale malt color. If you want something with a more luscious flavor and a deep copper hue, then you would use a crystal malt from the top end of the color range.

Careful selection and proportioning of crystal malts give you a lot of room to maneuver in recipe design. If you know the color of the malt, you can calculate how much you need to give your beer a particular color. You'll find a talk by Byron Burch very helpful for this (*Beer and Brewing*, Vol. 7, 1987, pp. 21–370. Boulder: Brewers Publications, 1987), although George Fix will tell you it isn't quite so simple (*zymurgy*, Vol. 11, No. 3, pp. 30–33)!

You can make a crystal malt substitute simply by toasting pale malt in an oven for 10 minutes at 350 degrees F (175 degrees C), as recommended by Charlie Papazian (*The Complete Joy of Home Brewing*. New York City: Avon Books, 1984). Or, you can get more complicated and make genuine crystal malts, as described by Randy Mosher (*zymurgy*, Vol. 11, No. 2, pp. 42–44). If you're prepared to do the extra work this is a good way to go, since it gives you the opportunity to experiment even more widely, and truly to come up with your very own version of pale ale.

Wheat Malt. Here we have a malt which can hardly be described as a traditional pale ale ingredient. In fact, if you use too much of it, you won't have a pale ale at all, but a new style of wheat beer! However, when used in small proportions (up to about 5 percent of the grist, or about four ounces per five gallons) it will improve the beer's head retention. This can be very desirable for a low-carbonated draught beer, which does not form a big head to begin with.

Analyzing malt at Young's Brewery, London.

A typical analysis for a wheat malt is:

Moisture: 4–6%
Nitrogen: 2–2.3%
Color: 1.8–3 °L
Extract: 80–82%; 36–38 °specific gravity per pound
per gallon.

This malt must be mashed along with the pale malt and, like pale malt, your yield of extract will probably be lower than the maximum quoted above. That will make little difference when used in such small proportions. Wheat malt is fairly high in enzymes, so there will be no problem in converting its starch. As you can see from its analysis, it will have virtually no effect on beer color, either.

Wheat malt should be readily available from your

41

supplier. It may come from several sources: English, German or possibly American. No matter what the source, its properties are quite similar; any differences can be ignored when used in the amounts recommended above.

Malt Extract. This is the alternative "workhorse" to pale malt if you do not wish to mash from grain. I haven't put it this low in the batting order because of any suggestion that extract brewing results in inferior beer compared to grain brewing.

It is difficult to know where to start in describing extracts. They are all proprietary products, and few if any manufacturers give complete analyses of their products in terms of color, extract, fermentability, etc. Even the descriptive names used may be quite vague or even misleading. Some are designed as virtually complete kits with hops already added (often in the form of hop extract), while others are straight malt extracts, either designed for a particular beer style or as a basis on which to build your own recipes.

You see, malt extract is really a concentrated wort. The manufacturer mashes pale malt along with any roasted malts or adjuncts he considers fit the style, then concentrates the wort by vacuum evaporation. Before evaporation the wort may be boiled to obtain the break, especially if will be a hopped extract. Depending upon the end purpose, the pale malt may be a lager, pale ale or amber malt. Also, the mashing temperatures will have been adjusted to give the desired level of fermentable sugars, so that the final gravity will vary from extract to extract.

You have probably already worked with malt extracts and have some idea as to which of them suit various beer styles, as well as your own style of brewing. I can only suggest that, if you still have doubts, you (a) consult with your supplier, and (b) use an extract designed for bitter, light or pale ale. The term "amber" can be misleading since, although some of these are designed for ales, others are meant for lager production. If you stick to British manufacturers, whose products are widely available, you can avoid this problem.

The best source of information on malt extracts is the magazine *zymurgy* (Special 1986, Vol. 9, No. 4, pp. 22–23; Winter 1985, Vol. 8, No. 5, pp. 30–31; Spring 1986, Vol. 9, No. 1, p. 22). In particular, these issues list hop rates (in HBUs) of the main brands sold in the United States. There is also some information on the types of barley from which the extract is made. A further article (*zymurgy*, Spring 1988, Vol. 11, No. 1, pp. 37–38) details the starting and finishing gravities obtained with standard brews from 12 "light" malt extracts. Despite the name, these included several amber-colored extracts which would be suitable for brewing pale ale.

Most malt extract syrups will give an extract of about 36 degrees specific gravity per pound per gallon, the corresponding figure for dry powders being 45 degrees specific gravity per pound per gallon. If the extract is already hopped, then most of the work has been done for you and there is less opportunity to put your own imprint on the beer. Other than that, there is nothing wrong with using these extracts except that they are sometimes underhopped by true pale ale standards. Just don't forget that they are already hopped, and allow for that before adding more!

In the recipe section I shall stick to unhopped, for simplicity's sake. There is really not much to choose between syrups and powders in terms of brewing quality. Powders are, however, sometimes simpler to use when a recipe requires quantities other than those in the syrup cans.

It is not an argument to get into here, but some brewers contend that extracts produce beers which are a little lacking in malt body and character, as compared to full-mash beers. If you agree with that and haven't yet found a solution to this problem, the answer is quite simple. Do a fairly crude mash of a couple pounds or so of pale malt and add the resulting wort to your brewpot along with the malt extract. Many extract brewers find this fairly easy to do, and well worth the little extra it adds to their beer. This will be covered further in the recipe section.

Please note that you must boil your wort for one to 1 1/2 hours, no matter what the manufacturer or anyone else says. I repeat that a high hop bitterness is the outstanding characteristic of this beer. As will be discussed under "hops," the levels of bitterness given in the recipes are based on the assumption that you get good utilization of the hops added. This can only happen if you have a proper boiling time, preferably with the full wort volume. If you have a shorter boiling time the beer is going to lack the required bitterness and you will be disappointed in it.

- Adjuncts -

Sugar. I am going to be brief here because, as discussed earlier, I do not think sugar has any place in the brewing of quality beers, except for priming. If you should have trouble with the formation of chill-hazes and have not kept the beer too cold, then you might want to experiment with the use of sugar as a nitrogen diluent. If so, remember that it is usually fully fermentable and will tend to make the beer taste thin. Its use should be limited to no more than 10 to 15 percent of the total grist.

Until fairly recently British brewers used either cane sugar (sucrose, a disaccharide) or invert sugar (an equal mixture of fructose and dextrose, both monosaccharides). Invert is usually prepared by hydrolysis of sucrose. Nowadays, the trend is to use syrups prepared by hydrolysis of starch, which typically consist mainly of glucose (dextrose) and maltose (a disaccharide). Corn sugar is produced in this way, but the hydrolysis has been taken to completion so that it is virtually pure dextrose.

If you must use sugar in your pale ale, stick to corn or cane sugar. Contrary to common homebrewing opinion, the latter will not give your brew a cidery flavor. Its bad reputation comes from bad brewing technique—using too much sugar and not enough malt, so that the beer is far too thin.

As far as extract is concerned, cane sugar will yield 45 degrees specific gravity per pound per gallon. Corn sugar gives less extract—about 36 degrees specific gravity per pound per gallon. For the record, cane sugar is not directly fermentable by yeast, but the latter contains enough enzymes to rapidly hydrolyze it to fully fermentable monosaccharides.

Flaked Maize. Like sugar, this is often used by British brewers as a nitrogen diluent in amounts of about 10 to 15 percent of the grist. Higher proportions may result in the corn flavor being detectable in the beer, which is most undesirable in a pale ale! Try it if you wish. It will improve the head retention of the beer a little, so perhaps it is a marginally better adjunct than sugar.

Flaked maize or corn is produced by dry-milling the grain to separate the endosperm from the skin and the germ. The larger particles of the starchy endosperm are separated and recovered as corn grits, which are sometimes used directly in American brewing. The grits are moistened with live steam and passed through "flaking rolls," where they are flattened into flakes. The starch content of the flakes is gelatinized by the heat generated in this process.

This means that flaked maize, unlike other cereal adjuncts, does not require cooking before mashing. But note that it consists largely of unconverted starch, so it *must* be mashed to be of any use in the brewing. Since it contains no amylolytic enzymes it can only be mashed with pale malt, so it is no use adding flaked maize to a straight extract brew. Typical extract levels are about 36 degrees specific gravity per pound per gallon. The reason that flaked maize can be used as a nitrogen diluent is that, although it is a natural cereal starch, it yields much less soluble nitrogen than pale malt. Finally, its use will add no color to the beer.

Other cereal adjuncts are used in commercial brewing, but usually require precooking to gelatinize the starch before mashing. None of these, including rice, flaked barley, sorghum or whatever, has any place in brewing pale ale. Note that wheat flour is sometimes offered as an adjunct; this is merely dehusked wheat malt and should be used as described under that heading.

- Hops -

Hops, of course, are where the heart of pale ale lies. Although bitterness is their most important contribution, aroma and hop character should not be forgotten. However, the latter aspect is not an essential part of pale ale flavor and aroma, as discussed in the style profiles (See Chapter 3). Many excellent bitters and pale ales are

Early springtime preparation of an English hopyard.

brewed without the use of aroma hops. On the other hand, since the levels of bitterness are high, pale ales, especially when brewed to low original gravities, can be rather one-dimensional.

As with wines, complexity generally makes for better, more interesting and well-balanced beers. Therefore the better pale ales, and anything designed to be something more than just a "session" beer, will benefit from the addition of hop character and aroma. It is a matter of opinion but, for me, the finest examples of the style do have this attribute.

Since it is optional, you can either late-hop or dry-hop. And you can use really any aroma hop you like. In British brewing, Goldings have traditionally been regarded as the finest pale ale hop both for bittering and dry-hopping (which is carried out in the cask for draught beers). But some very fine British bitters and pale ales are brewed from European aromatic hops. The newer English high-alpha hops, such as Wye Progress, Target, and Challenger, are also good aroma hops and have made inroads into what was formerly Goldings territory. Many American aroma hops also are suited to this purpose.

Goldings is no longer the only bittering hop for pale ale, either. These hops, sometimes called East Kent Goldings after the area where the best of them are grown, have a fairly low alpha-acid content, between 4 and 6 percent. Since alpha acid is what gives the bitter flavor, "high-alpha" hops from almost any source should be suitable replacements for Goldings and are likely to be more economical for us if they are American varieties. For example, I have had excellent results with Eroica (~12 percent alpha) and Galena (~14 percent alpha) as bittering hops in both bitter and pale ale.

In fact, genuine English Goldings are not easy to obtain in the United States, especially in loose form. That is because American suppliers find it hard to lay their hands on loose Goldings in good, fresh condition. This is an *extremely* important point. With a beer where hop bitterness is such a dominant part of its flavor spectrum, it is essential that this should be a very "clean" bitterness. Any harsh or coarse notes in the bitterness will be immediately apparent on the palate, making the beer rough and disappointing.

It is difficult to define what it is that makes bitterness "clean" or "coarse" in terms of hop chemistry. But it is certain that old, oxidized hops will give rougher flavors than very fresh hops. The hops for pale ale should be as fresh as possible. If you live in the United States, this is a powerful argument in favor of American hops and against English Goldings.

One alternative is to use pellets instead of loose hops. It is debatable whether pellets are as good when it comes to aroma, but there is no question about their equivalence when they are to be used for bittering. Goldings pellets are available in the United States, although you may have to look through a few suppliers' catalogs before you find them. An advantage of pellets, as far as the homebrewer is concerned, is that you can be pretty sure that they have been well-kept and are fresh and unoxidized.

One of the reasons that I love pale ale so much is because it is a hoppy beer. Hops are amazing in what they can do for a brew. You have to use only a small amount, and you can add all sorts of wonderful, intriguing flavors to the brew. Pale ale allows you to use these qualities to the fullest, and I urge you to experiment with all kinds of varieties, added at almost all stages of the brewing process. Use them for bittering, late hopping, fermentation hopping, dry hopping, with a single or several varieties, or with varieties you've never heard of before, but *use* them and your pale ales will never be dull or boring.

My personal preference is still Goldings for both bittering and dry hopping of draught pale ales and bitters. The full, yet not overpowering character of the Golding seems to me to be perfectly suited to this style. However, the table on page 50 lists a number of varieties which can be used for pale ales, along with recommendations as to where in the process they should be used and, where applicable, what they will do for the beer's aroma.

This table is not meant to be comprehensive. There are other varieties which are or may become available. I would particularly like to see the newer English high-alpha/fine-aroma varieties on sale here. It is ironic that one of the world's hoppiest beers, pale ale, is English, and yet English homebrew suppliers seem to know little about their own hop varieties and even less about the proper way to store hops. English malt extracts may dominate the U.S. homebrewing scene, but their hops are hard to find.

Variety	Origin	Alpha acid%	Bitter-ing	Aroma
Bullion	U.S.	8–10	Yes	No; too coarse.
Brewers Gold	U.S.	8–10	Yes	No; too coarse.
Cluster	U.S.	6–8	Yes	No; too coarse.
Cascade	U.S.	5–6	No	Yes; flowery.
Eroica	U.S.	11–13	Yes	Yes; resiny
Fuggles/ Willamette	U.S.	4–6	No	Yes; vegetal
Fuggles	England	4–4.5	No	Yes; grassy
Galena	U.S.	11–14	Yes	Yes; very resiny
Goldings	England	4–6	Yes	Yes; light floral
Hallertauer	U.S.	5–6	No	Yes; spicy
Hallertauer	W. Germ.	7–8	Yes	Yes; spicy
Northern Brewer	U.S.	9.5–10.5	Yes	Yes; highly vegetal
Saaz	Czech.	6.5–8.5	Yes	Yes; spicy/resiny
Styrian Goldings	Yugoslavia	6–8	Yes	Yes; resiny/floral
Talisman	U.S.	7–9	Yes	Yes; resiny
Tettnanger	U.S.	5–6	Yes	Yes; spicy

You should also bear in mind that new varieties are constantly coming onto the market. There are some very good suppliers in the United States who are always on the lookout for new developments, and sometimes have new varieties to offer to the amateur as soon as they are commercially available. It is well worth searching out these suppliers, and experimenting with any new hops they may introduce.

- Yeast -

It should be obvious by now that this style of beer requires a top-fermenting ale yeast. But it is not so obvious what that really means. No yeast can ferment if it is on top of the wort, and there are many ale yeasts with a wide variety of both physical and chemical properties.

Perhaps the simplest definition of an ale yeast in brewing terms is one that is only capable of fermenting sugars at temperatures above about 55 degrees F (13 degrees C). Virtually any yeast that fits this criterion is called top-fermenting, but *no* yeast ferments on top of the wort. Whatever the type of yeast, fermentation can only occur while the yeast is suspended in the wort. The difference between top- and bottom-fermenting yeasts is that, after primary fermentation is complete, top-fermenting yeasts rise to the surface and bottom-fermenting yeasts settle to the bottom of the fermenter.

Both yeasts form a rocky head in the initial stages of fermentation, and bottom yeasts always sediment out. Top yeasts may partially sediment, but are characterized by the formation of a "skin" on the surface of the green beer. Even highly flocculent top-fermenting yeasts, which tend to separate out from the beer before fermentation is complete, will form this skin. The ability of top-fermenting yeasts to do this is very important, since it means that open fermenters can be used with minimal risk of bacterial infection. Such fermenters are still used by British traditional brewers, despite the rise in popularity of closed conical fermenters.

51

In lager brewing it is now standard practice to use a pure strain, cultured from a single cell. Many ale yeasts are actually mixtures of two or more strains. This is often essential to ensure both a rapid fermentation and high attenuation. Another important characteristic of ale yeasts, which is partly a function of fermentation temperature, is the production of small amounts of esters in addition to alcohol. These esters are responsible for the fruity flavor and aroma in ales. It is one of the beer world's oddities that what is an off-flavor in a pale lager is a desirable characteristic in a pale ale!

What this means is that you need a true, preferably English, top-fermenting brewers yeast. It should be a strain or mixture of strains which will work well in whatever fermentation system you have, just as the Burton strains work best in the Union System. If the yeast settles out too quickly and you have no means to recirculate it, you may find it difficult to get proper attenuation of the beer.

That's the ideal situation, of course. In practice we have to work with what we've got. So let us review the options available to you. The first is that of using dried yeasts, which are readily available in a fairly wide variety. These are usually labelled simply as "Ale Yeast," and are the cheapest and easiest to use for the homebrewer.

Unfortunately, many of these yeasts are derived from baker's yeasts rather than from brewing strains. If so, they may give attenuation problems. Baker's yeasts are not accustomed to operating in high alcohol environments, and easily give up the ghost. Those dried types which are true brewing yeasts will give satisfactory results, although you should still be selective. Some of them are designed for "kit" brewing. In other words, they are used primarily for their ease of handling. They will usually attenuate fairly well, but then settle out rapidly, rarely forming the skin on the beer's surface that is so typical of a true top-fermenting yeast. Without that skin the beer must be racked quickly if you are using an open fermenter, and protected from the atmosphere to prevent infections.

Some dried yeasts also have a tendency to overdo the ester production, giving the beer an excessively fruity or even coarse flavor. Nevertheless, in recent years the quality of dry yeasts offered by brewing suppliers has dramatically improved. Talk to your supplier, tell him that you are brewing a pale ale, and he should be able to give you a yeast that will give good results.

I suppose dried ale yeasts are the brewing equivalent of the winemaker's "All-purpose Yeast." They are generally selected to give acceptable results with a wide range of beers—pale and mild ales, strong ales, porters and stouts—so that they rarely give outstanding results with one particular style. This brings us to a second option. No quality winemaker today would dream of using anything other than a carefully selected yeast culture, nor would any commercial brewer use anything else. Why shouldn't we be just as particular in our choice of yeast? It is astonishing how many homebrewers will pay through the nose for the best malt and hops, yet pick up the first packet of yeast they see on the shelf!

You can now obtain cultures of brewing strains fairly easily. Most good suppliers stock a range which includes ale yeasts. One or two even offer cultures from particular breweries or brewing areas, such as Burton. They are more expensive than dried yeasts, but I think the improvement they will make in your beer is well worth having. In any case, with careful technique you can reduce costs by repitching the yeast from one brew to another. Some suppliers offer a fairly inexpensive kit which will enable you to do this without much risk of infection. It is also possible, once you have decided that you really like the results achieved with a particular strain, to reculture it yourself. This is fairly tricky to do, and will be discussed below.

A problem with cultures, whether as "slants" on agar gel or as liquids, is that the samples you buy often will not contain enough viable yeast to ferment a five-gallon batch of wort. You must first make a starter and get the yeast actively working in a small volume of wort before adding it to the bulk. It is preferable to start with about one-half pint of wort, get the yeast going, double the volume, get that going, then redouble a couple of times more so that you have about one-half gallon of active starter to pitch in to your wort. Obviously, you have to time your starter production so that it is ready just as soon as your wort is ready.

Timing is less of a problem than the risk of introducing infection into your beer with the starter. This is a definite disadvantage of using a culture. If you have any doubts about your ability to prepare a clean, uninfected starter, for whatever reason, stick to using dried yeast.

Whatever your choice, you are still faced with the fact that there is only a limited number of yeast strains available. If you want to try other strains you will have to go to one of the brewing industry's sources, such as England's National Yeast Culture Collection, held by the Brewing Research Foundation. This will be a much more expensive proposition, and you have to know exactly what you want when you order.

Therefore, a third option is to collect your own brewing yeasts. Samples can often be picked up from friendly microbreweries; just make sure they brew pale ales and not lagers! If you're really lucky and live close enough to get a regular supply, you can pitch your wort with fresh yeast every time.

Another alternative is to use the sediment from a bottle of naturally conditioned pale ale, of which there are a few around. The technique is simple enough—just drink the beer and make a starter from the sediment. This approach is fraught with danger, however, apart from the usual risks involved in starter preparation. First, the sediment may not be the actual yeast used in that beer's brewing process. This may have been removed and replaced by a very different strain more suited to bottle conditioning. That classic pale ale, Worthington White Shield, actually uses a bottom-fermenting yeast for conditioning. From personal experience, it does not work well as a primary yeast for pale ale.

Second, the sediment may contain little active yeast, making preparation difficult and slow, thus increasing the risk of infection. In the case of some sedimented imported beers, they may have been pasteurized so that the yeast is completely dead. Find out if this is the case before you leave yourself with five gallons of wort ready for pitching and a completely lifeless starter!

Third, such sediments may carry infection, particularly if it is an old sample of the brew, as is all too often the case with imports. That doesn't necessarily mean that the brewery has been careless. True sterility is impossible in a brewery, so there can easily be one or two wild yeast cells in a bottle of naturally conditioned beer. Once the brewing yeast has done its conditioning and settled out, such wild yeast has no competition and can start to multiply and produce its off-flavors. This will rarely cause a problem if the beer is drunk within a month or two of bottling. But it can be serious if the beer has been around for several months or more.

Therefore, if you want to use yeast from bottle sediments be careful! Make sure it is really the yeast you want and that the beer in the bottle is as fresh as possible. If the beer itself does not quite taste right, don't use the yeast. If the yeast isn't very active and the starter is slow to get going, discard it! It would be a good idea to have some dried yeast in reserve before attempting this approach. It's always a disaster when your beer gets infected, but it's an even bigger disaster when it happens as the result of using a complicated technique which is supposed to improve your beer!

Finally, if you do get into collecting yeasts from breweries and bottle sediments, you'll probably want to maintain a bank of those samples you like best. You will have to make your own cultures for this, growing a small quantity on an agar slant in a tube and storing it in a refrigerator until required for use. This is a complicated and difficult technique, requiring absolute cleanliness to keep out unwanted microorganisms. It is not a technique I would recommend anyone to try, but if you really want to have a go at it, read Rog Leistad's book *Yeast Culturing for the Homebrewer* (Ann Arbor: G. W. Kent, Inc., 1983) or *zymurgy* Special 1989 (Vol. 12, No. 4).

- Water -

Water, of course, is the main ingredient of beer, as far as quantity is concerned. Since we do not generally want to taste it in our beer, it can be looked on as nothing more than a carrier for the things we do want to taste. However, naturally occurring water is far from pure in a chemical sense, containing, among other things, a wide range of dissolved minerals. As a result, it is not neutral in its effect on the taste of beer, nor is it neutral in its effect on the many complex reactions that make up the brewing process.

In fact, the chemistry of natural waters is very intricate, and it would be impossible to deal with it here in detail. What follows is only a very brief summary of the effects of its most important constituents as far as pale ale brewing is concerned. If you want more detail, consult Gregory Noonan's *Brewing Lager Beer* (Boulder: Brewers Publications, 1986), *Malting and Brewing Science*, by J.S. Hough, D.E. Briggs, R. Stevens and T.W. Young (New York: Chapman and Hall, 1982) or Darryl Richman's article "Water Treatment: How to Calculate Salt Adjustment" (*zymurgy* Winter 1989, Vol. 12, No. 5).

In a sense, homebrewers attach far too much importance to the quality of their brewing water. It is often difficult or even impossible to make major changes in the nature of the water supplied to your home. For many brewers, unless they can afford to bring water in from elsewhere, they have to brew with what they have or not brew at all. However, this is overstating the case a little bit. A little tinkering with the mineral content of the water can help make it more suitable for brewing a particular beer style.

As you know, the character of the local water had a lot do with particular areas achieving reputations as the best places for brewing particular beer styles. Burton, naturally, was the Mecca for pale ales, so we need to look at what is in Burton water that makes it so good. We cannot tell what actual minerals are there, because when they dissolve they break up into their constituent ions. It is the ionic content of the water that is obtained by analysis; what minerals were dissolved can only be inferred. Before we go any further, I must point out that I shall give all water analyses in units of parts per million (ppm; mg per liter). There are several other units used in the water industry, but most of them are more complicated and less clear to an outsider than ppm. Here is a typical analysis of Burton brewing water (listing only the most important ions):

ION	CONCENTRATION, ppm
Calcium	270
Magnesium	60
Sodium	30
Bicarbonate	200
Sulfate	640
Chloride	40

This water has around 1200 ppm of total dissolved solids, and a pH of 7.0 to 7.2. Most natural potable waters have much lower total solids. Burton water is high in permanent hardness because of the high calcium and sulphate content, but it also has a lot of temporary hardness from a high level of bicarbonate.

The ionic content of the water is of major importance in assuring that the mash pH is in the right range for optimum action of the starch-degrading enzymes. If it is not, extract yields will be low and undesirables like silica and tannins will be extracted into the wort. The optimum pH range is 5.0 to 5.5 and is achieved through several pH-controlling, or "buffering," reactions, largely involving calcium, with phosphate ions and acidic groups on polypeptide protein residues.

The main ions controlling these buffer reactions are calcium and sulphate, which drive pH down to the required level, and bicarbonate, which drives pH up to more alkaline levels. Bicarbonate is in fact much more effective at pushing up pH than the other two are at bringing it down. In dark beers, the roasted malts used are high enough in acidity to override the effects of bicarbonate. In pale ales there is not enough acidity in the grist to do this, and the pH depends entirely on the ionic content of the water.

Therefore, pale ale brewing generally requires water that is very low in bicarbonate, preferably below 50 ppm. But Burton water does not fit that criterion, does it? The reason is that it is extremely high in calcium and sulphate, so that there is enough of these two ions to bring down the pH, even with so much bicarbonate present. This is the real reason why the addition of gypsum to brewing liquor is known as "Burtonisation." Burton brewers did not invent the technique of water treatment!

There is more to water quality than just control of mash pH. Certain ions also affect beer flavor, their effect being more pronounced in pale than in dark beers. Sulfate is very important in this respect, imparting a dryness to the beer which accentuates the hop bitterness in a pale ale. If overdone, sulphate can taste harsh and bitter, however.

Burton water also contains sodium and chloride ions. These contribute both fullness and mouth feel to the beer, which helps add some complexity in the case of pale ales, although their effect is reduced by the presence of high levels of sulphate. If present in large amounts, sodium and chloride will make the beer taste salty, which is usually undesirable.

Magnesium ions are similar in effect to calcium ions as far as pH is concerned. At concentrations below about 30 ppm, magnesium also enhances dryness of the beer. Above this level it tends to impart an unpleasant astringency, as well as a laxative effect! Note that Burton water breaks this rule, with twice this amount of magnesium present.

Calcium and magnesium ions also have beneficial effects on other parts of the brewing process. The presence of calcium ions in the boil is essential to good break formation; i.e., precipitation of proteins and other materials which might otherwise cause beer haze formation. Magnesium, on the other hand, is an essential trace element in yeast metabolism, helping to ensure healthy growth.

Summing up, Burton brewing water is quite unique. Because of the complexity of water chemistry, you will almost certainly not be able to duplicate it by treating your own water supply. But you can, in most cases, adjust the content of the major ionic constituents that were discussed above and so have water well-suited to the brewing of high-quality pale ale.

Again, it is impossible to deal in depth with the wide range of water supplies across the whole of the United States. All that can be done is to lay out some guidelines. You should start by obtaining a full water analysis. If you are on a public supply, the utility company should provide this free. If you have a well, you will have to pay for an analysis at a local laboratory. The point is, you cannot sensibly treat the water unless you know what is already in it.

If the water contains high levels of organic materials, particulate matter, or excessive amounts of iron, it may be necessary to pretreat it by carbon filtration and/or ion exchange. If you do not want to get into the expense of that approach, you could obtain bottled water. That itself is probably mineralized, so will still need adjustment.

By the way, extract brewers may be thinking that they do not need to change their supply. After all, the mashing has already been done by the manufacturer, who will have taken care to adjust the mineral content of his water. Why should it be necessary to make any further adjustments? As far as the brewing process is concerned, it probably is not necessary. But as far as flavor is concerned, you might well want to increase sulphate and chloride levels.

Your water supply will fall into one of three broad categories: soft (less than 100 ppm total dissolved solids); medium hard (100 to 400 ppm t.d s.); and very hard (400 to 600 ppm t.d.s.). Soft is the ideal for our purposes, because you can adjust it to suit whatever type of brew you want.

Hard water is more of a problem. There are two types of hardness—permanent and temporary. Permanent hardness is caused by calcium and magnesium and is unaffected by boiling. This is obviously good for pale ale. Temporary hardness is caused by bicarbonate, which is reduced by boiling. Bicarbonate levels should be kept down for this style of beer.

In order to adjust your own water supply you have to know your goals. These should be your target concentrations for pale ale:

ION	ppm
Calcium	100–200
Magnesium	10–30
Sodium	10–20
Bicarbonate	50 maximum
Sulfate	300–500
Chloride	20–40

You cannot adjust the individual ionic concentrations separately. You can only add or remove salts, which are combinations of ions. For example, you can reduce bicarbonate, but only by converting it to calcium carbonate so that calcium is lost too. To increase calcium, you would add gypsum, a form of calcium sulphate, but then sulphate concentration would also be increased. This is why it is so difficult to adjust one natural water to match another.

Let's look at how to go about changing your own supply. I cannot tell you exactly what to do, but I can give you a framework to build on. First, let's take bicarbonate. This will likely be above the 50 ppm I have suggested. It is easily removed by boiling your mashing/brewing water before you start; on cooling, insoluble calcium carbonate precipitates out. Rack the water off the deposit and you are ready to go. This may seem like an unnecessary hassle, but if you are on a public supply it is probably well worth doing anyway, just to remove the chlorine. Chlorine can cause the formation of chlorophenols, especially if you are mashing, and these add some very unpleasant flavors to beer.

In fact, for a grain mash you have to heat up the water anyway, so why not take it up to boiling first? I always do, and I consider it good brewing practice. Remember, when you remove bicarbonate, you also remove calcium in the ratio of 100 ppm calcium to every 150 ppm bicarbonate removed. You will therefore probably have to add back that calcium in the form of gypsum (calcium sulphate).

Gypsum has the chemical formula $CaSO_4 \cdot 2H_2O$. This means that dissolving one gram in one gallon of water will give about 60 ppm calcium and about 150 ppm sulphate. Therefore, if you were starting with distilled water (which contains no dissolved ions), you would add three grams of gypsum per gallon to get 180 ppm calcium and 450 ppm sulphate—right at the top end of our recommended range. That is 15 grams per five gallons. Such additions are best weighed accurately. If you do not have a gram scale, work on the basis that one level measuring teaspoon is approximately five grams. Remember to scale down this amount according to the levels of calcium and sulphate already present in the water.

The amounts we are working with come close to the maximum solubility of gypsum in water. Further, gypsum has the unusual property of being less soluble in hot water than in cold. Therefore, add it to cooled water, and use plenty of agitation. In the case of extract brewing, make sure that you add only enough for the volume of water added to the boil and not for the whole brew length, if you cannot boil the whole brew length in one go.

If you are mashing you have another way to check whether you have added the right amount of gypsum. So long as you have removed bicarbonate, your mash should have pH 5.0 to 5.5. If it is higher than this, you need more gypsum.

Magnesium is added in the form of Epsom salts ($MgSO_4 \cdot 7H_2O$). Therefore, one gram per gallon will give 26 ppm magnesium and about 100 ppm sulphate. That is as much as you need according to our specification. Since this is five grams per five gallons, or one teaspoon in five gallons, this must be the absolute maximum you ever add! Epsom salts are very soluble in water, so you have no problem there. Remember that you get a lot of sulphate ion for a small amount of magnesium. So, if you do make an adjustment with Epsom salts, remember to allow for this sulphate in calculating your gypsum additions.

Sodium and chloride are adjusted by the addition of common salt, NaCl. Only small amounts are required. Just one gram in five gallons will give 20 ppm sodium and 30 ppm chloride. That is almost exactly the limit of our specification, so if you already have both these ions in your water, you are probably better off not adding any more. If your water already has higher levels of these ions than specified, there is little you can do about it except live with it.

- Finings -

These are not strictly an ingredient, but they are an important addition to the beer if you want to brew a traditional, cask-conditioned pale ale. They are certainly not necessary if you bottle the brew and are not essential if you are kegging it, especially if you are prepared to let the beer mature several weeks before drinking it. But if you want to drink kegged beer quickly, or if you are putting it into a wooden cask where it is essential that it be ready to drink quickly, you should add finings.

"Finings" is brewing jargon for any clarification agent used in the process. It includes copper finings (added to the boiling kettle, or "copper") such as carrageenan, or Irish Moss, which is added in the last 10 to 20 minutes of the wort boil to help ensure good break formation. In British pale ale brewing the term is more specifically applied to an isinglass solution used to sediment yeast in a cask-conditioned beer.

Properly applied, isinglass not only ensures rapid settling of the yeast but also helps to form a compact sediment which is not disturbed when the beer is drawn off from the cask. With the help of finings, beer can be drunk just as soon as it has come into condition rather than waiting several more days before it clarifies.

Isinglass is an extract of the swim bladder of certain fish. That doesn't sound too pleasant, but it is basically just collagen, a material similar to gelatin but of much higher molecular weight. This allows it to bind several yeast particles together, so that they are heavier and settle much more rapidly than if they were still individual particles.

Isinglass finings are readily available. Your supplier should be able to get them if they aren't already in stock. You can use them according to the instructions on the packet. I prefer to make my own solutions. Simply crumble five grams of isinglass powder into one pint of water, add five grams tartaric acid (or winemaker's "acid blend") and one gram sodium metabisulphite. Store in a tightly stoppered bottle. Store the bottle in a refrigerator, shaking it three to four times a day for two to three days.

Note that fining solutions must be kept below 70 degrees F (21 degrees C) or they will rapidly deteriorate and lose their effectiveness. For a typical bitter or pale ale, they should be added at the rate of six ounces of the above solution to five gallons of beer. They should be thoroughly mixed with one pint of beer before adding to the bulk (along with the primings) when the beer is racked into the cask or keg. The beer should be stored at room or cellar temperature while fining and conditioning, and should be ready to drink within one week after casking.

EQUIPMENT

- General -

This is going to be a very short section, on the assumption that you are already a brewer and therefore have the basics on hand. Pale ale brewing requires no special equipment for the actual brewing process. In other words, when using malt extract you need a brewpot, preferably large enough to boil the whole brew length. If mashing you need a similar pot for stove mashing, which can also double for boiling. If you are stove mashing, you will need a lauter-tun, perhaps equipped with a grain bag, for separation of the wort from the spent grain.

If you are using a type of picnic-cooler mashing system, you can use this for wort runoff and sparging as well—a separate lauter-tun is not necessary. Microbrewers, too, can runoff directly from the mash-tun.

Naturally, you must have a primary fermenter as well. If you use a true top-fermenting yeast, then a simple, open fermenter will work perfectly well. Such fermenters are still widely used by the more traditional British brewers. If you prefer to use a closed fermenter, that's fine too. Many of you are using the blowoff type of arrangement, which is also fine, although some hop bitterness may be lost with this technique. One other comment I have on this stems from the fact that a number of homebrewers seem to think this operates just like the Burton Union System. It does not at all.

In the blowoff apparatus, anything that blows off is lost entirely, including a fair amount of iso-alpha-acids. These are the bittering substances in beer, which also have significant foam-forming properties. The Union System, in contrast, recirculates the blown-off beer. The aim of the Union System is to allow separation of a very powdery, non-flocculent yeast from the beer. There are many merits to the blowoff setup, but it is *not* a Burton Union by any stretch of the imagination.

Kegging and casking warrant some comment. Although pale ale is generally regarded as being a bottled beer, I am firmly of the opinion that it is at its best as a low-carbonated draught beer. Therefore, you may want to serve it this way. Kegging is easy, and offers several alternatives. There are a variety of plastic vessels on the market, usually of British origin, designed for the serving of naturally conditioned beer. Most of them provide for carbon-dioxide dispensing of the beer but, carefully used, they should not result in overcarbonation. Their major disadvantage is that they are difficult to cool, even to pale ale drinking temperatures.

If you are prepared to spend more money, the stainless-steel soda kegs are an even better system. These are widely available from brewing suppliers, together with all ancillary equipment. These too depend on carbon dioxide dispensing of the beer. With careful use of the regulators that come with these systems, it is possible to dispense the beer at carbonation levels close to one volume. The design of these kegs also lends itself to easy cooling, even during the hottest summer.

You can also use a proper brewing keg, if you can lay your hands on one. The dispensers are readily available from brewing suppliers. These kegs are air-operated, which has the disadvantage that the beer must be consumed quickly or it will spoil. Their advantage is that they cannot overcarbonate the beer, and in that respect they are similar to a traditional English cask.

- The Cask -

Finally, we come to the cask. It is thought that beer was first bottled in England some three hundred years ago. But bottling did not become common commercial practice until around the beginning of this century, and is now on the decline. The British, and especially the English, consider that their beer is at its best when served on draught. For the purist, as exemplified by the CAMRA membership, that is not enough, for the beer must also be

The traditional wooden cask.

conditioned in the cask and served without the application of external carbon-dioxide pressure.

Before we go any further, we have to define what the English mean by the word "cask," since it has no particular significance in American usage. In the United States, draught vessels are commonly called "kegs," but an English keg is quite different from a cask. The latter is barrel-shaped, which means that the sides are arched, with the flat, circular ends, or heads, fitting into a groove inset from the end of the sides. A small bung-hole (about one inch in diameter) is situated in one of the heads, and is normally fitted with a brass bushing, known as the keystone. In the middle of the arched side, in a plane diametrically opposed to the bung hole, is a much larger hole about two inches in diameter. This is known as the shive hole, and is also usually fitted with a brass collar.

Beer is served from the cask through a tap fitted into the keystone, being replaced by air drawn in through a hole in the shive.

Traditionally, casks were made of wood. Though some brewers still prefer this material, most modern casks are made of lined aluminium or stainless steel, though the arched, barrel shape is retained. Kegs, on the other hand, are made only from metal and are cylindrical in shape. Unlike a cask, a keg has only one hole, which is in the center of the head. In use the keg stands on one end, with the sealed hole at the top. A "spear" fitting is inserted into the hole, reaching to the bottom of the keg. This fitting essentially consists of two concentric tubes. The beer is driven up one of the tubes and out of the keg by carbon-dioxide pressure applied to the other tube. The beer can *only* be dispensed by externally applied pressure, so that air never comes into contact with it and spoilage is not a problem if the beer is slow in selling.

"**Real Ale**" vs. "**Keg**". The most significant differ-ence between the two systems is that of conditioning. Real ale is primed with sugar at racking, and undergoes a secondary fermentation in the cask, which means that the yeast cannot be filtered out. It will have a fairly low CO_2 content (0.75 to 1.0 volumes), which is *not* aug-mented during serving. In fact, since air enters the cask as beer is drawn off, the gas content of the beer actually drops a little during dispense. Because ale yeasts cease to ferment sugar below about 50 degrees F (10 degrees C), the beer has to be conditioned at 50 to 55 degrees F (10 to 13 degrees C), and is therefore usually served at this tem-perature as well.

Keg beer is normally chilled, filtered, pasteurized, and artificially carbonated. Typical CO_2 contents are 1.5 to 2.0 volumes, and this may increase during serving as the beer absorbs some of the gas used to force it out of the keg. Since no fermentation takes place in the keg, such beers often are stored and served at temperatures below 50 degrees F (10 degrees C).

Keg beers offer the commercial brewer the advantage that careless publicans and barmen can do little to spoil the beer. Real ale requires a good deal of skill and attention to ensure that it is at its best when served. Even if it is properly handled, it can quickly spoil through oxidation or the action of airborne organisms, because it may take several days to empty the cask after it is broached.

Unfortunately, filtering and pasteurization both spoil the flavor of keg beer. What little is left is finally killed off by the high gas level in the beer, which alters its pH as well as making it fizzy. Real ale in prime condition retains all its flavor, and its low gas level means that every bit of this flavor makes its impact on the drinker's palate. American drinkers, used to lagers with high gas contents, often find this difficult to believe. It is not unusual for English pubs to serve similar or even identical beers in both keg and cask. If you ever get the chance to visit England, find such a pub and sample both beers alongside each other. Just a mouthful or two should convince you that the keg beer is bland and gassy, while the real ale is a beer of character and distinction.

While much real ale is served in metal casks, the real purist will tell you that wood is best. Indeed, a Society For The Preservation Of Beers From The Wood was in existence in England for years before CAMRA came into being. The argument is that wood, because it is porous, harbors microflora such as Brettanomyces, which can improve the flavor of the beer still further. Some drinkers go so far as to say that it is possible to discern differences in flavor when the same beer is served from two different wooden casks. It is difficult to be sure if this true; whether served from wood or metal casks, real ale is never a constant, uniform product. The skill of the publican, the conditions of his cellar, the length of the secondary fermentation and the method of dispensing mean that even the contents of an individual cask, whether wood or metal, cover a range of flavors. Much of the charm of real ale lies in the fact that it is never entirely predictable. That may not be to the liking of the big brewer, who wants his brands to be instantly recognizable, but it is exactly suited to the real beer-lover who wants his beverage to be a constant source of both mystery and pleasure.

More About Wooden Casks . First, the wood itself. Ideally, this should be English oak, but this is scarce and expensive these days, and most new cask wood is either German or Polish oak. Apparently, only oak has sufficient density (when properly cut) to ensure that the cask will be fully watertight under pressure. Additionally, only English, German, and Polish oak do not impart flavor to the beer. American oak, in contrast, is unsuitable, since the beer will leach out various undesirable flavors from it. As a matter of record, many "new" English casks are not made from new wood, but are assembled from reconditioned staves taken from old casks.

The man who makes a cask is called a cooper, and he learns his skills during a four-year apprenticeship. Coopering is a craft which goes back to antiquity. The Cooper's Company, a tradesman's guild, was established in England in 1307. The advent of the bottle and metal casks and kegs has meant a decline in the number of coopers, but there are still over a thousand of them in Britain today. The majority of these are employed in Scotland in the whisky industry, with perhaps a couple of hundred or so brewers' coopers left in England. Most of these work for individual

71

breweries, repairing and reconditioning the brewery's stock of casks. There is only one independent brewers' cooper left—H. & J.E. Buckley Ltd., Dukinfield, Cheshire.

The sides of a cask are made up of a number of planks, or "staves." These are tapered on the sides and from the center to each end so that they will fit tightly together. Initially they are straight, and are assembled in a circle at one end by means of a hoop, or "chime." They are then wetted, and a small fire of oak shavings is kindled within the circle of the chime. This makes the wood pliable, so that two strong metal hoops can be fitted over them, about one-third of the way from each end, thus forcing the staves into tight contact with one another. The ends of the staves are then trimmed off, and a groove is cut all the way around the inside, at both ends, about one inch from the end. The circular heads, consisting of several pieces of oak closely mated together by means of dowels, are inserted into these grooves. Holes are then cut in one head and in the belly, the brass keystone and shive seatings are inserted, and the cask is ready for use.

The art of the cooper lies in the fact that he makes only two measurements—the length of the staves and the diameter of the head. All the rest is done by a combination of hand and eye, with what appears to be almost casual deftness. The result is a strong, durable container that will remain watertight under moderate pressure, and which will stand up to fairly rough handling for many years. Its great strength comes from its double arch construction, with the staves forming an arch from head to head and around the heads, so that they reinforce each other in two different planes.

Casks come in various sizes, based on the "barrel," which is 36 Imperial gallons (43.2 U.S. gallons; 163.4 l). The "pin" (4.5 Imperial gallons; 5.4 U.S. gallons; 20.4 l), and the "firkin" (9 Imperial gallons; 10.8 U.S. gallons; 40.9 l) are the sizes most suited to homebrewers' needs, though if you want something bigger there is also the "kilderkin" (18 Imperial gallons; 21.6 U.S. gallons; 81.7 l). These last three names are of Dutch origin, reflecting the fact that it was Dutch and Flemish immigrants who introduced hopped beer to England.

It is not easy to come by used casks, even in Britain; it is probably undesirable to do so anyway, unless you are sure the cask has been properly looked after. A neglected wooden cask is very difficult, perhaps even impossible to get properly clean. You will almost certainly be better off buying a new one. The only source I know of is H. & J.E.

A cooper making casks in the Samuel Smith cooper shop.

73

Buckley Ltd., Tame Valley Works, Park Road, Dukinfield, Cheshire, SK16 5LP, England. Buckley's casks are also advertised as being available through Corfield Associates (UK), 360 Queens Avenue, London, Ontario, Canada.

Cleaning Wooden Casks. The great disadvantage of a wooden cask is that it is difficult to clean. It is also difficult to keep it clean if it is used only infrequently. A new cask should have been treated with bisulphite before shipping, and should require only a cold water rinse before use. In fact, by the time you get the cask, the staves will have dried out and shrunk somewhat during shipping, so that it is no longer watertight. You will therefore have to soak the cask with cold water until the staves have absorbed enough water to swell and reseal themselves.

All that you have to do is to bung off the keystone, fill the cask with cold water, and leave it. Top off with fresh water to replace any leakage; how often you have to do this depends on how much the cask has dried out. In any case, within one to four days, the leakage should have stopped and you can go on to the next stage. Actually, I prefer to soak with the addition of about two teaspoonfuls of metabisulphite or, better still, an ounce of household bleach (the unperfumed type) per five gallons of water, to inhibit bacterial growth.

Once the cask has finished soaking, empty it and refill with the dilute solution of bleach described above. Note that I said "refill," not "rinse." Empty the cask and refill it with clean, hot water. Repeat these two steps once or twice more and the cask is ready for use. Don't worry about the bleach tainting the beer; so long as you use only the dilute solution quoted above and rinse the cask thoroughly this will not be a problem.

If you do decide to go with a used cask, much sterner measures are required. You will need to soak it with a solution of strong detergent/sterilizer, such as Chempro SDP, for one-half to one hour. Empty it, hose it out thoroughly, then give it three or four fill/empty cycles with cold water before finally treating it with bleach, as described above for a new cask. If you want to be sure the cask is fully clean you can conduct a dummy fermentation, using sugar solution with added nutrient and yeast, as described by Dave Line in *The Big Book Of Brewing*. Personally, I feel that this isn't worth the effort. If you are still doubtful at this stage, I would advise you to throw the cask away and go buy a new one! Serving beer from the wood requires a lot of extra effort and expense, as compared to bottling, and it's hardly worth it if you finish up with an infected beer.

One final point. Once you have your cask cleaned and in use, keep it clean and do not allow it to dry out. When you empty it of beer, hose it out with cold water, fill it with the dilute bleach solution and keep it topped up until you are ready to fill it with another brew.

Further Equipment. Shives—these are wooden bungs for the keystone and shive hole. That for the keystone is called a "tut," and comes with a wide hole cut halfway through it, so that a tap can be forced into it, knocking out the bottom half, and leaving just a narrow collar around the tap to ensure a seal. The much larger shive has a small hole drilled through its center. The hole can be knocked through so that spiles can be fitted in the shive. A supply of both types of shive can be purchased along with the cask.

Spiles—there are two types of these wooden pegs: porous and hard. The porous is made from bamboo, and permits the exit of gas and foam from the cask. The hard spile is non-porous and seals the cask when hammered into the shive. Both types can be purchased from the manufacturer. Get a good supply; they should be used only once.

Clump hammer—this is a device for removing old shives. It is impossible to describe so, if you want one, ask the shive manufacturer. You can do the same job a little more messily with a wood chisel and hammer.

Stillage—because of its shape, a cask must be supported to prevent it rolling around. All kinds of things have been used as stillage, the simplest form being wooden wedges. Place one on each side of the cask, close to the hoop, with a third at the rear of the cask. A popular form of stillage is the cradle. Two pieces of wood are joined to form an "X"; these are joined to another "X" by a series of cross pieces, so that the cask can sit snugly in the top half of each "X". Basically, you can use anything you want for stillage, so long as it holds the cask firmly in position. It should permit the keystone head to sit slightly lower than the rear head, so that as much beer as possible may be withdrawn from the cask.

Taps—these come in wood, stainless steel, or brass. The wooden ones are readily available in the United States, and are inexpensive. Unfortunately, they tend to leak, especially as the beer comes into condition. Once they start to leak they are subject to mold growth. At this point, they become a dangerous source of infection and should not be reused. Metal taps are much superior in this respect, but are expensive and hard to find. For gravity dispense, you need a racking or bottling tap, which turns down at the end. If you intend to use a beer engine (hand pump) to dispense the beer, you'll have to find a tap with a threaded end, either double or single, so that you can screw on a hose fitting. Be careful though, as threads are very variable. It looks as if each beer-engine manufacturer uses his own thread pitch! You are probably better off

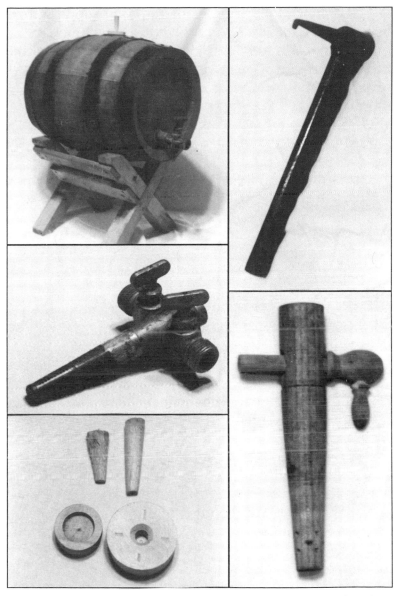

Equipment for wooden casks (clockwise from top left): tapped cask on cradle (stillage) with shive and spile at top; clump hammer; wooden tap; soft and hard spiles, tut and shive; brass two-way tap (for beer engines).

buying a new tap from your hand-pump supplier than buying an old tap and hoping its thread will match.

Mallet—you will need a wooden mallet to drive home the shives. The round-head type is best, and is readily available from hardware stores or camping suppliers.

- Casking and Conditioning of Beer -

It is possible, if you wish, to cask after secondary fermentation. In this case, the beer will be fairly flat, and you will need a little more priming sugar, which often results in a vigorous in-cask fermentation with much frothing through the spile. In fact, English brewers generally rack into cask right after the primary stage, and I prefer to do the same. There will be a secondary fermentation in the cask, anyway. This approach requires only a small amount of priming sugar, and is slower and more controlled. If desired, the beer can be racked, fined, and left to stand a couple of days before racking into the cask. Provided your yeast is not powdery and nonflocculent, I think you will find it easier to clarify the beer if the finings are actually added to the cask. Once you have some experience in handling casked beer, you'll be able to decide which approach you prefer.

The first thing you must do with your clean cask is to fit the tut, hammering it tightly home in the keystone. In England, the publican fits the tap into the tut when the beer has conditioned. This is not at all easy to do without losing a good deal of beer! Since it is not really necessary for the homebrewer to do this, it is recommended that the tap should be fitted before filling the cask with beer. You can drive the tap shank through the tut with the aid of the mallet, but this often results in the tut splitting, with subsequent leakage of beer. You will find it easier to cut out the center of the tut with a chisel, then drive the tap firmly into position.

Place the tapped cask on its stillage and rack the beer into it through the shive hole until it is about half-full. Thoroughly stir the finings (six ounces of 1 percent isinglass, as described in Chapter 4) into about a pint of beer and stir thoroughly with a clean plastic spoon. Add this mixture to the cask along with the primings (two ounces cane sugar, 2 1/2 ounces corn sugar as syrup). Rack the remainder of the beer into the cask, filling flush to the bottom of the brass collar and no higher. Push a shive into the hole, make sure it is straight, and pound it tightly into position with the mallet.

Now we are ready for the conditioning. Knock out the center of the shive with a screwdriver or nail set and gently tap in a soft spile. The spile should sit firmly enough to make a seal, but not so tightly that it cannot be removed by hand. Now the cask and its contents need to be kept at 50 to 55 degrees F (10 to 13 degrees C) if possible.

Temperatures above this range are bad, not only from the point of view of flavor, but because excessive frothing through the spile may occur, resulting in loss of beer. One way around this is to use the blowoff fermentation technique. Remove the spile and fit a length of quarter-inch plastic tubing into the shive, making sure that it does not go in so far that it enters the beer. Put the other end into a bottle containing dilute metabisulphite or bleach solution.

The best approach is to control the fermentation by cooling, but in warmer climates this is no easy matter. Perhaps the only simple method is to drape the cask with wet sacking. This is fairly messy, as the sacking must be *kept* wet. A refinement of this is to drape bags of ice over the sides of the cask and on top of the sacking, perforating the bottom of the bags so that the melt water keeps the sacking wet. If you can think of a better method use it, and let me know about it!

As the conditioning fermentation gets under way, there will be some frothing through the spile. Providing this is not excessive, simply wipe it off at regular intervals so that beer does not run down the side of the cask and invite attack from spoilage organisms. As the frothing subsides, the porous spile must be replaced by a hard peg. Exactly when to do this is something that can be learned only by experience. Thirty-six to 48 hours after the start of conditioning is usually about right, but this can vary greatly according to temperature, finishing and starting gravity, yeast strain, etc.

Once the hard spile is in place, the beer should be left for a few more days until it has fallen clear. Do not be too eager to sample it. There is little head pressure in a cask, so you have to remove the hard spile to draw off beer. That will let air in. If the beer is not yet clear you cannot re-spile it and wait till it is clear or it may have spoiled. Again, only experience will tell you when you have reached the right moment to broach the cask.

In order to vent the cask for serving, remove the spile completely, either by gently knocking it from side to side with the mallet or pulling it out with a pair of pliers. There is only a low level of carbonation in the beer, so serving it through the tap by gravity alone will result in minimal head formation. This can be improved by opening the tap wide, and holding the glass well below the tap until it is nearly full. The hard peg should be replaced after each serving, to avoid loss of condition.

When the cask is about one-half to one-third full, tilt it gently towards the tap by means of a wedge at the back;

this will ensure that you can draw off the maximum amount of beer. Do not overdo the tilting, however, or you may disturb the yeast sediment and make the beer cloudy.

You should empty the cask within two to three days of broaching it. If you keep it longer, it will almost certainly become infected and spoiled from the air which is now present in the cask. Even if infection is avoided, longer keeping will result in the beer losing its condition and becoming flat and lifeless.

There is no substitute for experience in learning how to properly handle beer from the wood. The ability to serve a perfectly conditioned pint from a cask is an art. Do not be discouraged if you cannot get it right the first few times. A failure or two will only make it all the sweeter when you do get it right. And when you do draw off from the cask a beautifully clear, sparkling glass of your finest IPA, take a good mouthful, and reflect on the fact that you are drinking it just the way those thirsty soldiers in the Indian Army would have drunk it a century or more ago!

- The Beer Engine -

This is the proper name for the dispensing equipment colloquially known as a "handpump." The latter name comes from the fact that it is operated by a handpull, or pump handle, which sits on top of the bar. These are usually about 12 to 18 inches long and sit vertically on top of the bar. They are often made of china and brass, decorated with hunting scenes, and usually carry a pumpclip announcing the brew offered from that pump. If several traditional brews are available they will sit in one or more banks on the bar, making a wonderfully welcome sight to the true real-ale lover.

You do not need a beer engine to serve beer from the wood. It is a device invented for the pub, where the beer is kept in a cellar some distance away from the bar, and must be lifted from the cellar to the point of dispense. However, if you are really into cask beer it is a nice extra touch, especially at parties.

Naturally a beer engine will cost you more money. England is the only place where they are still made in any quantity. You can buy old ones in England but they are not that easy to find, and there is also the problem of associated fittings, as I mentioned earlier. In the United States I think your best bet is to buy a new one and take the supplier's advice on fittings such as hose connections, cask taps, etc. Perhaps even more importantly, they will also be able to provide you with spare washers for the engine and the cask fittings, which may otherwise be impossible to find. Your initial outlay for a new engine may be quite a bit more than for a used one, but I think you will find it cheaper in the long run. I am speaking from experience when I say that. I bought a pair of old pumps and I don't even want to try to remember how much time and effort it took to renovate them and hunt down spares!

Two of the bigger English suppliers are Homark Associates, Pottery Road, Parkstone, Poole, Dorset, BH14 8RB; and Hi-Gene Beer Pumps Ltd., 49, Storforth Lane Trading Estate, Hasland, Chesterfield, S41 0QR. CAMRA may also be able to help you in finding a suitable manufacturer, especially if you take out a membership with them!

The guts of the engine consist of a simple cylinder with a beer inlet at the bottom and an outlet at the top. This is fitted with a plunger that moves up the cylinder as the handle is pulled down. There is a flap valve in the top of the plunger. This valve stays closed as the plunger moves up the cylinder, pushing the beer out and through the dispense tap. When the cylinder is empty the handle is pushed back to the vertical position, which in turn pushes the plunger back to the bottom of the cylinder. As the plunger descends, the flap valve opens and the cylinder is refilled with beer, ready for the next pull on the handle. Normally, a single pull will deliver about one-half an English pint (10 ounces) of beer.

The whole unit requires careful mounting on a substantial base, as the diagram indicates. You will need a suitable length of reinforced nylon beer hose, and a couple of butterfly nuts and hose connectors so the cask tap can be connected to the inlet end of the engine. You should also have a stainless steel trough, which sits below the tap to collect spillage. I would also recommend that

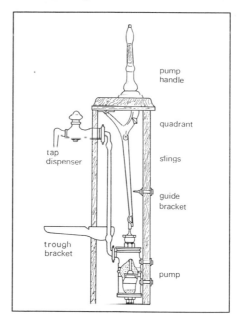

Beer engine.

you obtain the type of dispense tap which takes a "spar-kler" fitting. This little device screws onto the end of the tap and is essentially a restricted orifice that makes the beer flow turbulent. When screwed on tightly the spar-kler produces a big, tight head on the beer, which is how it is typically served in Northern England. When the sparkler is only loosely screwed on, a lesser, fluffier head is formed. Without the sparkler there is much less head formation. This is more typical of Southern England.

Serving with a beer engine is quite straightforward. Hold the glass under the tap, with the sparkler in the desired position, and give a slow steady pull on the handle, repeating as necessary, until the glass is full. It is a very satisfying thing to do when the beer is your own and you are serving it to appreciative friends. But some drinkers would say that one of the finest sights in the world is that of a buxom barmaid heaving on a handpull to serve you your first pint of the day!

PROCEDURES

- Extract Brewing -

The handling of extract is quite standard in brewing pale ale. Simply dissolve the extract after the water has been properly treated and proceed with the boil. Crystal malt should be mixed with a few pints of the water, which are then brought to a boil and the liquid strained into the bulk. If the partial mash technique is to be used, then include the crystal malt and flaked maize, if used, with the pale malt.

For the partial mash, you are concerned more with flavor than with achieving a high yield of extract. You do not have to be so thorough and painstaking as when carrying out a full-scale mash. That does not mean you can be sloppy, though. You have to grind the malt carefully, as described in the section on mashing. You will normally be working with two to three pounds (0.9 to 1.5 kg), depending upon the recipe.

Ideally, you should use one quart (0.95 l) of water per pound of malt. If you have not used this technique before you will find this makes quite a thick mash, which is hard to stir and easy to burn on a stove top! Therefore, for your first go you will be better off using 1.5 quarts (1.4 l) of water per pound of malt. This must be treated as per our discussion above, or as recommended in the recipe.

You want your mash to be at a relatively high temperature, say 153 to 155 degrees F (67 to 68 degrees C), since you are looking for dextrins and flavor, not extract. When you add the malt (at strike) there will be some cooling, so your water must be at a higher temperature; 160 to 163 degrees F (71 to 73 degrees C) should be about right.

Hold the mash at 153 to 155 degrees F (67 to 68 degrees C) for at least 30 minutes, and preferably 45 minutes to one hour, stirring vigorously to ensure an even temperature throughout the mash. At the end, raise the temperature to about 170 degrees F (77 degrees C) and strain off the liquid into your brewpot. Run a further two to three quarts of hot water at about the same temperature through the mass of grain. Then add the rest of the water you need for the boil, dissolve the extract, and away you go.

- Mashing -

The first thing you have to do is to crack the malt. This is relatively simple with British two-row pale malt, as discussed under "Ingredients." But "relatively" is the

85

operative word, for this is not so simple when you have to handle as much as eight to 10 pounds (3.6 to 4.5 kg) at a time, which will be the case for the higher-gravity pale ales. In fact, grinding the malt improperly can cause severe problems, especially for the amateur, who has a limited number of equipment options open to him.

If you undergrind, you will get poor starch conversion and low yields of fermentable extract. If you overgrind, then you will have too much fine material in the grain bed and wort runoff will be very slow. In really bad cases, the bed will become almost totally impermeable, and no liquid will pass through it at all. This is the condition known as a "set mash," and it is almost as much of a frustrating experience as sampling a new brew which turns out to be badly infected!

Most commercial brewers use a double grind. The first stage uses fairly wide-set rollers, which really only separate the husk from the malt kernel. A set of sieves separates out the husks, and the kernel is then lightly ground through a pair of more closely-set rollers in the second stage. This allows for sufficient grinding of the kernel to allow maximum extract yield, while keeping the husks intact so that the grain bed remains sufficiently permeable to permit rapid wort runoff.

Unless you make your own grain mill, you will almost certainly be using a piece of equipment which operates on the one-pass principle, such as a hand-cranked grain mill or an adapted coffee-grinder. If you fine grind to give maximum extract you will also crush the husks, and that means runoff problems. If you put it on a coarser setting, so as to leave the husks intact, you will lose extract yield. Believe me, this is the lesser of two evils. Once you have done a brew or two and know what yield you are getting, you can compensate simply by adding a little more malt the next time. If you have ever had a set mash, you will realize the power of this argument!

Crystal malt can be ground along with the pale malt. It is very friable, and presents no grinding problems. Starchy adjuncts like flaked maize require no grinding and should be added directly into the mash.

Pale ale mashes are quite uncomplicated. A simple infusion mash at the saccharification temperature of 150 degrees F (65.5 degrees C) is sufficient. The British pale malts now available in the United States are of excellent quality, and will give full conversion in one hour at this temperature, although the mash is best left for 1 1/2 hours to ensure full flavor development.

In fact, mashing at that temperature makes for a thin, highly fermentable beer. Especially for the lower-gravity bitters, this is not desirable, for the hop bitterness becomes too dominating. We want high attenuation, so that the hop bitterness comes through unmasked by sweetness, but we also need some dextrinous body to balance the bitterness. Some mouth feel is provided by the crystal malt, but we also need some dextrin contribution from the pale malt.

That means you should mash at slightly higher temperatures, preferably 151 to 155 degrees F (66 to 68 degrees C). Go to the higher end of this range for a heavily hopped, high-gravity IPA, and to the lower end for a low-gravity bitter, with pale ales somewhere in the middle. You will probably be using more crystal malt in a bitter, so will need less body contribution from the pale malt, whereas the reverse is true for IPA and pale ales.

You should use one quart (0.95 l) of water per pound of grist (i.e., pale and crystal malts, plus any starch adjuncts used). Treat the water as required, heat to 160 to 163 degrees F (71 to 73 degrees C), and add the grains.

Keep the mash at 151 to 155 degrees F (66 to 68 degrees C) for 1 1/2 hours, and check for starch conversion with iodine. If you have not achieved full conversion by this time, you never will! Raise the temperature to 170 degrees F (77 degrees C) to prevent further enzyme action, and you are ready to run off the wort.

As mentioned earlier, if you are using a mash-tun with a bottom runoff, such as the picnic-cooler type, you can collect the wort directly from the tun. If you are mashing in a pot on the stove, then you will have to transfer the mash to a lauter-tun for runoff. Sparge the wort with treated water at 170 to 175 degrees F (77 to 79 degrees C), always keeping the liquid level above the grain bed so that it does not dry out or form channels. You need enough water to yield about six gallons of wort for a five-gallon brew length (see under "Brewing," next section). To achieve maximum extract, runoff and sparge should take two to three hours, but that is usually impractical for the amateur, both in terms of time taken and the ability to control flow rates closely.

Do not oversparge! As the runoff drops in gravity, you can easily start to extract silicates and tannins and their polyphenol precursors from the spent grain. The former will cause hazes in the beer while the latter will make for harsh flavors, which will be very noticeable and objectionable in a pale ale. Once the runoff has dropped to an SG of around 1.010 (2.5 °P), stop collecting it. You may improve extract yield slightly by going further, but you will probably do so at the expense of beer stability and flavor.

- Brewing -

A properly conducted boil is an essential part of good brewing technique for any beer. In the case of pale ale, with its accent on hop bitterness, no corners can be cut. The boil must be vigorous, or "rolling," and must last a full 1 1/2 hours. The alpha acids of hops must be converted to iso-alpha-acids, which are the real bittering compounds in beers, to get their full effect. In wort this conversion is fairly slow. It is helped to completion by the high temperature and long time recommended.

Alpha acids are not very soluble in wort, and as the heat is increased the resins melt into large droplets. The swirling action of a rolling boil continually breaks up these droplets into much smaller ones, so that a much larger surface area is exposed. This ensures that maximum solubility of the alpha acids is attained and conversion to the desired iso-alpha-acids is taken as far as is possible.

Maximum conversion is achieved in about 1 1/2 hours. Commercial brewers utilize no more than 35 percent of the added alpha acid, and homebrewers can probably expect to manage no better than 25 to 35 percent utilization. Some iso-alpha-acids are lost during fermentation, because they have considerable surfactant activity. They are partly responsible for foam formation and are left behind as the foam subsides. You must face the fact that most of the alpha acids you carefully add to your brew will never even make it through the boil. Increasing the boil time beyond 1 1/2 hours will not improve alpha-acid utilization any further, either. So now you see why some brewers are so keen to bitter their beers with pre-isomerized hop extract.

As an aside here, it is worth noting that there is no precise relationship between hop bittering units (HBU) and International Bittering units (IBU). They are really two very different things. HBU is a measure of the alpha acids added to the boil, whereas IBU is the concentration in milligrams per liter (ppm) of iso-alpha-acids in the *beer itself.* Therefore, IBU is an analytically determined number and tells you exactly what is in the beer when you finish brewing. The difference between the two is a measure of the efficiency of *overall* brewing utilization, which includes fermentation losses.

If you know exactly what utilization you are going to get, you can relate the two directly. But that utilization depends both on how you carry out the boil and how you operate the fermentation, which will vary from brewer to brewer. In making any connection between HBU and IBU you must also remember that the first is a weight and the second is a concentration, so that units must be carefully defined.

If you assume a utilization of 20 percent, then IBU are approximately three times the total HBU in five gallons. At 25 percent then, 3.8 x HBU = IBU per five gallons. Throughout this book I have assumed you will get 20 to 25 percent utilization and used this in all my calculations, including the recipes. Microbrewers would be well-advised to do proper IBU analyses and determine their own utilization factors.

British brewers generally add their bittering hops just as the wort comes to the boil. You may do so too, if you wish. However, there is an argument that they should not be added until the first break has formed, after about 10 to 15 minutes boiling. The theory is that a significant portion of the alpha acids may be lost with the break particles if they are added at the start. Try adding the hops after 10 minutes boil, if you like. It will not do any harm and may improve your utilization slightly.

It has already been pointed out that there are no hard and fast rules as to which hops should be used for aroma, or whether hop aroma and character should be achieved by late or by dry hopping. English brewers use either, a combination of both or even none at all. Therefore, if you decide you want to late hop, there are no rules as to when you should do so.

You can add aroma hops anytime between the last 20 minutes of the boil and the end of boil. Basically, the earlier in the boil you add the aroma hops, the less aroma you will get in the finished beer because of the volatility of hop oil. However, if the addition is made while the wort is still boiling, some of the oil constituents, which are chemically very reactive, may be converted to non-volatile substances which will remain in the beer. The flavor they confer on it is usually referred to as hop character.

Early addition to the boil will result in more hop character than aroma. On the other hand, adding to the wort after the heat is turned off and boiling has ceased will result in more aroma than character. The latter, for the same hop variety, will be slightly different than for earlier addition. And, of course, dry hopping the final beer will result in a lot of aroma, with character very similar to the aroma.

Add all that to the wide range of hop varieties that can be used, *and* that a different variety can be added at each point, and the permutations are endless. It is, accordingly, impossible to make detailed recommendations other than those which will be given in the recipes. I hope the section on hops has already encouraged you to want to further explore these possibilities yourself, and to develop your own classic of the style.

Just a few comments on my own preferences. When late hopping with the traditional Golding, I find I get the best results if I them add at the end of the boil. The Golding aroma is not an overpowering one, and tends to

91

get lost if the hop is added during boiling, unlike some of the more spicy or floral hops such as Hallertauer or Cascade. Talisman gives an excellent hop character when added 10 to 15 minutes before the end of the boil, while Northern Brewer should be added for the last 20 minutes or its aroma may be much too pungent. Eroica, in contrast, although quite aromatic, seems to work well either in the boil or at the end.

- Fermentation -

Since we are using top-fermenting yeasts, fermentation temperatures should be kept at 60 to 68 degrees F (16 to 20 degrees C). Lower temperatures will make for too sluggish a reaction, and probably poor attenuation. Higher temperatures can be used and will certainly make for a rapid fermentation, with high attenuation. Going up to 72 degrees F (18 degrees C) will not cause any significant problems.

If you cannot control temperatures at these levels, you may still be able to produce acceptable beers at up to 80 degrees F (21 degrees C). But at these temperatures more esters will be produced and the beer will have excessively fruity overtones. More fusel oils or higher alcohols may also be formed; these will coarsen beer flavor (as well as making for bad hangovers).

High fermentation temperatures can affect beer flavor in other ways. They make for a rapid completion of the reaction and for lower solubility of carbon dioxide. If close attention is not paid to the beer, air can easily get in and cause oxidation, with the accompanying generation of stale, woody, and cardboardy flavors. If you are using an open fermenter, immediately after the primary fermentation is over the beer must be protected against the ingress of air, either by racking into a sealed container (which must be some kind of pressure vessel), racking into a secondary fermenter fitted with a one-way vent, or by using an airlock. In the case of a closed primary fermenter already fitted with an airlock or blowoff device, the fermenter must be topped up to reduce the empty space above the beer to a minimum.

"Warm" fermentations usually result in more vigorous foaming than lower temperatures. This is particularly true of pale ales, with their high levels of hop bitterness. The iso-alpha-acids responsible for this bitterness promote foam formation. The corollary of this is that these substances are lost to the beer as the foam subsides. Therefore, too high a fermentation temperature tends to result in low hop utilization and a beer lacking in both bitterness and head retention properties.

Furthermore, at elevated fermentation temperatures the rate of diacetyl production is increased. Commercial brewers pay a great deal of attention to obtaining low diacetyl levels, partly because diacetyl gives the beer a buttery flavor that is regarded as an objectionable note in many beer styles, and partly because it has a very low taste threshold (most people can detect it at well below one ppm concentration).

However, in this style of beer high diacetyl levels may not be a problem. To begin with, if you have fermented at a high temperature then you will almost certainly follow this with a period of warm storage in contact with the yeast at similar temperatures. This is a very effective way of reducing diacetyl concentrations.

Also, the flavor of diacetyl is not necessarily considered objectionable in a pale ale. Its flavor threshold is probably somewhat higher in a highly hopped ale than in a pale, light lager. Some pale ales, especially those fermented in Yorkshire Stone Squares, have a noticeable diacetyl flavor component which is often regarded as a desirable note in those particular beers!

Flavor is a subjective thing. If you like a buttery note in your beer then perhaps you should not be concerned about diacetyl production. If you do not like it, then control over fermentation temperatures is your best defense against it. Warm storage will reduce a good part of any diacetyl formed, but the lower the temperature during fermentation the less diacetyl that is produced in the first place.

Temperature control during fermentation is a perennial problem for the amateur in the United States, especially in those areas where ambient temperatures rarely go below 70 degrees F (21 degrees C). For those of us with cold winters, one way around the problem is simply to eliminate summer brewing. Even then, if you do not have a cool basement and have to brew in the house itself, you (or the other occupants) might not want to keep the house below 68 degrees F (20 degrees C) in the winter. It may be no accident that top fermentation flourishes in Britain, where anything over 70 degrees F (21 degrees C) is regarded as a heat wave!

English commercial brewers usually control their top-fermentation temperatures by means of a cooling coil in the vessel itself. Even in that climate this is necessary, because heat is generated during yeast reproduction. On a large scale, where this heat cannot easily escape, cooling must be applied to keep the temperature constant. On a five-gallon scale, the heat produced is not so much of a problem as is the heat picked up because of high ambient temperatures. That means that, unlike English brewers, U.S. brewers may need to apply cooling *throughout* the primary fermentation and not just intermittently.

Cooling of fermenting wort is not a problem home-brewers as a group have really solved. There is equipment available for almost every other stage of brewing, from mashing to filtration and kegging. The making of wort-coolers is well-documented in the literature, and ready-built versions are on sale if you do not want to construct your own. But for fermenter cooling there is nothing.

Perhaps this is because every situation requires its own approach, depending upon exactly where you live in a particular area, whether you want to brew year-round, whether you need to ferment the wort in a kitchen or whether you have a suitable basement or cellar available. Cooling an open fermenter can be done by means of a simple copper coil connected to the water supply, which is usually well below ambient temperature. However, if your ambient temperature is above the required fermentation temperature, you will have to run the cooling water continuously throughout the fermentation. That could significantly increase your brewing costs. You also have to make sure that your exit line is firmly fixed to a safe drainage point to avoid flooding.

Closed fermenters are a more difficult problem. Apart from anything else, it is extremely difficult to monitor the liquid temperature in a glass carboy without opening it. Perhaps the best solution is to stand the vessel in a bath of water within the desired temperature range. This may take a lot of water, for it will have to be replaced at regular intervals according to how hot a climate you live in. Standing the fermenter in the bath is not a very practical solution if it means that you cannot shower for five days when outside it is over 80 degrees F (27 degrees C)!

You must be careful, too, not to overcool the wort, or fermentation will be very slow and attenuation may not go far enough. Genuine top-fermenting yeasts just do not work very well, if at all, below 50 degrees F (10 degrees C). In fact, you are probably better off working at a temperature that is a little too high, rather than one that is too low.

Remember that you are looking for good attenuation with this style of beer. Secondary fermentation or long storage in the bottle or keg will help this, but it will not solve problems due to poor attenuation in the primary fermenter. One-fourth of the original gravity is the target for standard-gravity pale ales. In other words, we are looking for a finishing gravity no higher than 1.014 (3.5 °P) in the case of IPA, and perhaps as low as 1.008 (2.0 °P) in the case of a low-gravity bitter.

- Secondary Fermentation/Cellaring -

A secondary fermentation in the sense normally meant by homebrewers is not strictly necessary with this style of beer. In the production of real draught bitter in England, the green beer from the primary is generally racked directly into the cask and priming sugar is added, often along with finings. The cask may then be stored in the brewery for up to seven days at 55 to 60 degrees F (13 to 15.6 degrees C) before shipping to the pub. During this time the priming sugar ferments and the beer comes into condition. After a short period (one to three days) in the pub cellar, preferably at 50 to 55 degrees F (10 to 13 degrees C), conditioning and clarification are complete and the beer is ready for drinking.

It might be only semantics, but since it is priming sugar that is fermenting and since this is taking place in the beer's final storage container, it is not really a secondary fermentation. In contrast, "non-real" beers may be warm-stored at 55 to 60 degrees F (13 to 15.6 degrees C) in bulk. For keg beers and bottled beers, this may simply ensure completion of attenuation and remove more of the suspended yeast prior to chilling, filtering and pasteurization. If so, the warm storage period may be no more than a day or two, followed by several days at 35 to 40 degrees F (2 to 4 degrees C), during which time there is further separation of yeast, trub and chill-haze particles.

Certain high-quality, often high-gravity pale ales may receive a much longer period of warm storage, perhaps as much as several weeks. In this case there will be some secondary fermentation, if only through slow attack of the yeast on the lower dextrins. During such a period there will be flavor changes in the beer, as well as simple clarification by settling of suspended solids.

The general trend in commercial brewing throughout the world is to reduce maturation and lagering times, since this involves tying up a considerable amount of capital. For English brewers this is even more of a problem, since beer duty is payable at the time the wort is cast into the fermenters. It is hardly surprising that most pale ales and bitters receive a minimum amount of storage at the brewery nowadays. This does not mean that your beer will not benefit from maturation, however. We should always be prepared to learn from the professionals. Just remember that they *are* professionals, and they must make money, as well as beer!

Two to three weeks in secondary fermentation before bottling is fine, so long as all air is excluded. You could do the same with draught beer as well, if you wished. The only difference between U.S. draught beer and real ale is that no air is allowed into the draught container when the beer is dispensed. I therefore like to treat my draught beer as though it were real ale and rack it into the keg, along with finings and primings, straight from the primary fermenter. Unless things are desperate, the cask will stay undisturbed at cellar temperature for at least two to three weeks before the beer is drunk. High-gravity pale ales and IPAs can be left to mature for much longer periods.

Note that dry hopping in traditional English practice is carried out at the time the beer is racked into the cask. The hops may be added in loose form or as pellets. Nowadays, even the loose hops are added as a compressed block, so that they can be dropped in through the bung-hole of the cask. For the amateur, addition of loose hops can cause blockage of dispensing lines. If you prefer using these to pellets, simply put them in a nylon hop bag (available from most suppliers) and drop the bag inside the cask or keg.

It actually takes quite a long time (as much as three weeks) to extract *all* the oil of the dry hops into the beer. Most English traditional draught beer, dry-hopped or not, is consumed before that time. Therefore, if that is where you have previously encountered dry-hopped beer and you want to try it for yourself for the first time, be careful. If your beer has matured for several weeks, unlike the commercial English variety, you may get a much more powerful hop aroma than you expected!

Finally, note that however you decide to do your maturing of the beer, whether in a secondary fermenter, keg or cask, the storage temperature is important. You may take the beer up to about 70 degrees F (21 degrees C) for a week or so in order to get it into condition. Otherwise, maturation is best carried out at fairly cool temperatures. The ideal is 50 to 55 degrees F (10 degrees to 13 degrees C), since that is the typical temperature range in an English cellar. Top-fermenting yeasts are habituated to this environment and will continue to work, although somewhat slowly, until all the priming sugars are used up and the finished, fully conditioned beer is well-attenuated.

If you do dry hop your beer, you would be well-advised to avoid storing it at much above 65 degrees F (15 degrees C). Warmer temperatures will cause oxidation of the hop oils, especially if you have been at all careless about air getting into the beer while racking. This will result in the formation of off-flavors ranging from a woody to a "rancid-butter" aroma and flavor, depending upon the hop variety used.

- Packaging -

Much of this topic has already been dealt with under other headings. There are a few points that need to be covered, however. You have the choice of bottling, kegging or, for the more adventurous, casking. So long as you are relying on natural conditioning in each case then all three techniques are more or less authentic, if not entirely traditional. I assume you already know how to bottle and keg, so we shall not discuss those techniques except in the general discussion on carbonation levels below. Casking was dealt with earlier.

If you are filtering and artificially carbonating the beer, that is another story. Filtration is not impossible for the amateur working on a small scale (see, for example, Todd Hanson's "Home Filtration and Carbonation" in *Beer and Brewing Vol. 7*, pp. 93 to 117). This method has the advantage that, if properly done, it removes chill hazes as well as yeast and trub. Since it may also involve artificial carbonation, it can result in very low levels of dissolved air in the beer.

Apart from being non-traditional techniques, there are other arguments against filtration and artificial carbonation. Principally, filtration can remove larger proteinaceous molecules from the beer, and this can adversely affect both mouth feel and head retention. In addition, artificial carbonation often results in much higher gas levels than are suitable for the pale ale style.

For the homebrewer, since it is your beer and yours alone, you can do whatever suits you. I am not going to try and convince you either way. Just do not throw out traditional methods simply because of standards set by somebody else. But by all means use new techniques, if *you* think they give better results.

The microbrewer, on the other hand, may have to bow to other people's standards simply because he has to sell his beer to stay alive. He may have to sell into a market which has never seen a naturally conditioned bottle of beer, a market which itself has been conditioned to expect only bright, clear, highly gassy beer. So he may have to filter and carbonate just to survive. Many amateurs dream of opening their own brewery and selling their own classic brew. It can be done—a few have done it—but it is often next to impossible. Once a brewer has his plant up and running and has debts to pay, he all too often finds he has to brew what the public thinks it likes, and not what he wants to brew.

Because a beer going out into the retail market (especially in bottles) may sit two or three months before it is drunk, it may be considered necessary to pasteurize it. The yeast present in a naturally conditioned beer helps stabilize the beer against oxidation and limit bacterial growth. If the yeast has been filtered out, the beer has no such protection and can rapidly deteriorate. Pasteurization can kill both bacteria and wild yeasts, and prevent them from causing off-flavors in the beer. Unfortunately, it is very easy to overdo pasteurization, which will result in the beer having an unpleasant, "cooked" flavor.

Once, while judging pale ales in a competition, I gave low marks to the commercial standard which had been slipped in as a "sleeper" by the organizers. At the time, I had not been expecting a commercial brew and could not quite place the source of this strange flavor. When, at the end of the competition, I found out what the beer was, I immediately realized that it was the cooked note from a heavy-handed pasteurization.

A good alternative to pasteurization, and one which avoids the above pitfall, is sterile filtration. This requires a membrane with a pore size fine enough to filter out bacteria. It is a technique used by some of the larger brewers for their bottled "draft." I know at least one micro which also uses it, and they produce an excellent beer.

It is not a particularly simple technique. The membranes cannot handle a heavy load of suspended solids. A rough filtration must be carried out first, using standard techniques with diatomaceous earth. Once the beer has been sterile-filtered, great care must be taken that no infection is introduced in subsequent handling or the whole procedure will be negated. Nevertheless, brewers who believe pasteurization is just as likely to spoil a good beer as to improve it might find sterile filtration an acceptable alternative.

Now we should look at carbonation levels. I have already referred to the fact that pale ales are beers which are spoiled by too much carbon dioxide. I make no apologies for repeating myself on this score, for it is a fundamental point in appreciating the true greatness of pale ale. Whether you bring the beer into condition by priming, kraeusening, or artificial carbonation, *you must not overdo it!* Draught beers should contain 0.75 to 1.0 volumes, and bottled beers 1.5 to 2.0 volumes of carbon dioxide.

You must limit the amount of priming sugar to meet these specifications for naturally conditioned beers. Defining this amount is not so simple as it might appear, for the simple reason that we may not know the CO_2 content of the beer at final racking. If you have adhered to the strictures on fermentation temperatures and kept the green beer below 70 degrees F (21 degrees C), then it will probably contain about 0.5 to 0.7 volumes CO_2 at racking. Higher fermentation temperatures will mean lower gas levels.

If this is the case, you really do not need any more CO_2 for a draught beer. However we now have a problem. With anything other than a true cask system, you need some CO_2 pressure to drive the beer out of the keg. Since the beer is in equilibrium with the headspace at racking, you have to provide a little extra gas to drive it out. If you prime with two ounces of cane sugar in five gallons, you are adding about 0.8 volume CO_2, giving a final figure somewhere around 1.3 to 1.5 volumes.

This is too high for the style, according to our specifications. The catch is, you have no choice if you are to force the beer out of the keg. However, once some beer has been drawn off, a new equilibrium will be established between the beer and the larger empty space above it. This will result in a lowering of the gas content of the beer. Once again, a starting value of 1.5 volumes will not be enough to dispense a full five gallons of beer and more gas will have to be supplied to it.

To handle this see-saw problem, prime with only one to one-half ounces of cane sugar (or 1 1/4 to 1 3/4 ounces of corn sugar) per five gallons, and add extra gas as required, according to whatever keg system you are using. If you have one of the plastic kegs with extra CO_2 provided by means of a 16-gram bulb, simply fire in another bulb every time there is insufficient pressure to draw off another glass. You are still going to get variation in carbonation levels all the way to the end, but there is nothing you can do about that. In any case, there is a constant variation in the carbonation of a cask-conditioned beer once it has been opened for dispensing.

If you have the stainless-steel soda-keg system, complete with CO_2 cylinder and pressure gauges, life is more straightforward. You should again prime with a maximum of two ounces of cane, or 2 1/2 ounces corn sugar. As beer is drawn off you will need to supply more gas from the cylinder to continue dispensing the beer. Set your gauge as low as possible, two psi being the ideal. At this setting, and a temperature of 55 degrees F (13 degrees C), the beer will come to equilibrium at about 1.1 volumes. If you set the gauge at higher pressures, say five to 10 psi, and allow gas into the beer for just a few seconds to continue dispense, there will be no great increase in gas content. If you leave the gas line on continuously at these higher pressures, you will run the gas content up close to two volumes, which is not desirable.

The relationship between applied pressure and liquid concentration of a gas is a complicated one with a gas like carbon dioxide, which reacts chemically with water. It is not necessary to understand the mathematics of such a system in order to keep pale ale properly. Just remember, if gas is needed apply it only while dispensing beer and you will not go far wrong.

The situation is much simpler in the case of bottled beers, since we do not have to worry about changing pressures. If you prime five gallons of beer with three ounces of cane, or 3 3/4 ounces of corn sugar, at around 55 degrees F (13 degrees C), you will increase carbonation by about 1.2 volumes. Therefore, if you started off at 0.5

to 0.7 volumes the fully conditioned beer will contain 1.7 to 1.9 volumes, which is exactly where our specification says it should be.

- Serving -

The most important point here, after the subject of carbonation, is temperature. English beer should never be served "warm." On the other hand, it should never be served freezing cold, as so much American beer is served. No beer of character should be offered at close to freezing. English beer, and pale ale in particular, is best drunk cool, at cellar temperature. 50 degrees to 55 degrees F (10 degrees to 13 degrees C) is the ideal range. Anything higher than that tends towards revolting; anything lower tends to mask the flavor. Very low temperatures seem to lose the hop bitterness characteristic of this style completely.

This last point is important. I have tried English beers in the United States that have been served cold, and have been quite disappointed with them. In some cases I have even wondered whether nostalgia had taken over from fact and they really were not as good as I remembered. Then, on return to England, I sampled the same beer at the proper temperature and faith was restored as flavor came flooding back.

Frankly, I cannot accept the "lawn-mower beer" theory. Sure, there are times when I am sweating and want something which is only cold and wet. That's when I go for a soda. When I want a beer, I want it served the way its brewer intended it to be served and not with its heart frozen out of it. That applies to a good lager beer just as much as to a pale ale.

Finally, enjoyment of a beer depends on the drinking environment as well as on the quality of the beer. Just as

an Alt is best drunk in Düsseldorf, or a Pilsner in Plzeň, so a pale ale shows at its finest when drunk in England. If you really want to appreciate the style you have to try it in a real pub, over a game of darts or cribbage, or accompanying a discussion on the vagaries of the English climate. Or even better, with a chunk of Stilton, or a pork pie and mushy peas.

4

Pale Ale Recipes

In this section, three recipes will be given for each example. One will be on a one-barrel (1.17 hl) scale, and two will be on the five-gallon (18.9 l) scale, with one each for extract and mashing methods. This does not mean the three beers will be identical, just that they will be very similar.

In order to avoid repetition, metric units will be quoted only as the *direct* conversion of the standard U.S. unit. If you brew solely on the metric system, you will probably want to round off the brew length to a whole number. If you do so, do not forget to factor all the ingredients to your new base.

In determining original gravities in grain mashing, I have assumed a pale-malt extract of 30 degrees specific gravity per pound per gallon for the five-gallon brews, and 35 degrees specific gravity per pound per gallon for the one-barrel brew length. If your own extract figures differ from these you will have to add more or less pale malt accordingly.

Because of the complications of water treatment, recommendations are made only as to the desired levels of calcium, sulfate, and chloride ions. Actual additions of gypsum and sodium chloride will have to be worked out according to what is already in your water supply, as described in the section on water. Do remember that bicarbonate levels may have to be reduced by boiling the water before mashing.

For the sake of convenience, boiling time is assumed to be 1 1/2 hours in every case. Bittering hops are always added at the start of boiling, as discussed in the section on brewing. In converting HBU to IBU, I have assumed a 25 percent utilization factor for the small-scale brews. In the case of the one-barrel recipe, the microbrewer should get closer to 30 percent utilization. This is the figure used for those recipes. If you have had your beer analyzed for Bittering Units, you will know your exact utilization factor and should use this to recalculate hop rates.

Palates attuned to American beers may find the suggested bitterness levels rather high. You may, of course, reduce them if you wish. Do not be in a hurry to do so, however. The basis for determining these levels is that the beer should fit the classic definition of the style. Please see what the beer tastes like at that level. If it seems too bitter at first, drink some more and let your palate get used to it! Hop bitterness is a major part of this beer's character and surely we *do* want to brew beers of character?

It is assumed that you are using a top-fermenting yeast. Specific cultures will not generally be recommended, since their use depends on both availability and your own capability to handle yeast cultures. Fermentation temperatures will be kept in the range of 60 to 68 degrees F (16 to 20 degrees C), as discussed in the section on fermentation.

How you dispense the beer is up to you, but recommendations as to whether a particular beer should

Pump handles in an english pub.

be bottled or served on draught will be made. For simplicity, it is assumed that all conditioning is achieved through fermentation of priming sugars. If you wish to filter and artificially carbonate, read the discussion in the appropriate section. Please, please do not serve any of these beers cold! Keep the beer as close to 50 to 55 degrees F (10 to 13 degrees C) as possible. If you find that is too warm for you, either keep drinking it that way until you get used to it or give up trying to brew genuine pale ale!

Although these are tried-and-true recipes and you are encouraged to use them "as is," you should not regard them in any way as limiting, apart from the strictures on bittering and serving. Rather, the recipes should be seen as a starting point from which you will experiment to produce your own versions of the style. I will always be pleased to hear from anyone wanting me to sample a pale ale, IPA or bitter brewed to a recipe which they think is better than any of those listed here!

109

STANDARD PALE ALE

Amount	5 gallons (Grain)	5 gallons (Extract)	1 barrel (Grain)
British pale malt (2.5 °L):	8 lb (3.6 kg)	——	42.5 lb (19.3 kg)
Crystal Malt (60 °L):	2 oz (57 g)	2 oz (57 g)	0.75 lb (340 g)
Pale malt syrup:	——	6 lb (2.7 kg)	——
Pale dry extract:	——	0.5 lb (227 g)	——
Color (°L):	~10	~10	~8
Bittering hops			
Goldings (5% alpha):	1.75 oz (50 g)	1.75 oz (50 g)	9 oz (255 g)
HBU:	8.8	8.8	45
IBU:	32.8	32.8	32.6
Aroma hops			
Goldings (end of boil):	0.5 oz (14 g)	0.5 oz (14 g)	3 oz (85 g)

Water treatment:	Calcium 150 ppm; Sulfate 400 ppm; Chloride 40 ppm.
Mash temperature:	150°–152° F (65.6°–66.7° C)
Original gravity:	1.048 (11.8 °P)
Finishing gravity:	1.010–1.012 (2.5–3.0 °P)
Priming sugar:	3 oz (85 g) cane sugar, as syrup, in 5 gallons.
CO_2 (volumes):	1.5–2.0
Packaging:	In bottle.

Note: In the extract brew, add the crystal malt to two pints of water. Bring to boiling, strain off the grains and add the liquid to the main brew.

BEYOND THE PALE PALE ALE

Amount	5 gallons (Grain)	5 gallons (Extract)	1 barrel (Grain)
British pale malt (2.5 °L):	8.3 lb (3.8 kg)	——	44.3 lb (20.1 kg)
Crystal malt (20 °L):	4 oz (113 g)	4 oz (113 g)	1.6 lb (0.73 kg)
Pale malt syrup:	——	6 lb (2.7 kg)	——
Pale dry extract:	——	0.75 lb (340 g)	——
Color (°L):	~7	~7	~6
Bittering hops			
Talisman (8% alpha):	1.3 oz (37 g)	1.3 oz (37 g)	6.6 oz (187 g)
HBU:	10.4	10.4	53
IBU:	39	39	38
Aroma hops			
Hallertauer (10 min.):	0.5 oz (14 g)	0.5 oz (14 g)	3 oz. (85 g)
Cascades (end of boil):	0.3 oz (9 g)	0.3 oz (9 g)	2 oz (57 g)

Water treatment:	Calcium 180 ppm; Sulfate 450 ppm; Chloride 40 ppm.
Mash temperature:	151°–153° F (66.1°–67.2° C)
Original gravity:	1.050 (12.3 °P)
Finishing gravity:	1.011 1.013 (2.75–3.25 °P)
Priming sugar:	3 oz. (85 g) cane sugar, as syrup, in 5 gallons.
CO_2 (volumes):	1.5–2.0
Packaging:	In bottle.

Note: In the extract brew, treat crystal malt as in previous recipe.

ANGLO-AMERICAN PALE ALE

Amount	5 gallons (Grain)	5 gallons (Extract)	1 barrel (Grain)
British pale malt (2.5 °L):	7.7 lb (3.5 kg)	——	40.7 lb (18.5 kg)
Crystal malt (60 °L):	6 oz (170 g)	6 oz (170 g)	2.3 lb (1.0 kg)
Pale malt syrup:	——	6 lb (2.7 kg)	——
Pale dry extract:	——	5 oz (142 g)	——
Color (°L):	~10	~10	~9
Bittering hops			
Brewer's Gold (9% alpha)	0.75 oz (21 g)	0.75 oz (21 g)	3.8 oz. (108 g)
HBU:	6.8	6.8	34
IBU:	25	25	24.8
Aroma hops			
Fuggles (end of boil):	0.5 oz (14 g)	0.5 oz (14 g)	3 oz (85 g)
Goldings (dry hop):	0.3 oz (9 g)	0.3 oz (9 g)	2 oz (57 g)

Water treatment:	Calcium 120 ppm; Sulfate 350 ppm; Chloride 30 ppm.
Mash temperature:	150°–152° F (65.6°–66.7° C)
Original gravity:	1.046 (11.3 °P)
Finishing gravity:	1.009–1.011 (2.25–2.75 °P)
Priming sugar:	2 oz (57 g) cane sugar, as syrup, in 5 gallons.
CO_2 (volumes):	1–1.3
Packaging:	Draught only.

Note: In the extract brew, add the crystal malt to two quarts water, bring just to a boil, strain off the grains and add liquid to the main brew.

YER AVRIDGE BITTER

Amount	5 gallons (Grain)	5 gallons (Extract)	1 barrel (Grain)
British pale malt (2.5 °L):	6.1 lb (2.8 kg)	——	32.2 lb (14.6 kg)
Crystal malt (80 °L):	8 oz (227 g)	8 oz (227 g)	3 lb (1.4 kg)
Pale malt syrup:	——	5 lb (2.3 kg)	——
Pale dry extract:	——	0.3 lb (136 g)	——
Color (°L):	~13	~13	~12
Bittering hops			
Northern Brewer (10% alpha):	0.75 oz. (21 g)	0.75 oz. (21 g)	3.75 oz. (106 g)
HBU:	7.5	7.5	37.5
IBU:	28	28	27

Water treatment:	Calcium 100 ppm; Sulfate 300 ppm; Chloride 30 ppm.
Mash temperature:	150°–151° F (65.6°–66.1° C)
Original gravity:	1.039 (9.7 °P)
Finishing gravity:	1.008–1.010 (2.0–2.5 °P)
Priming sugar:	1.5–2 oz (43–57 g) cane sugar, as syrup, in 5 gallons.
CO_2 (volumes):	0.8–1.2
Packaging:	Draught—there really is no other way for a bitter!

Note (i): In the extract brew, treat the crystal malt as in Anglo-American Pale Ale.

Note (ii): If you like this brew, repeat it with one-half ounce (14 g) dry-hopped Goldings and see what you think of that!

113

PRIDE OF MILFORD BITTER

Amount	5 gallons (Grain)	5 gallons (Extract)	1 barrel (Grain)
British pale malt (2.5 °L):	6.75 lb (3.1 kg)	1.5 lb (0.68 kg)	36 lb (16.3 kg)
Wheat malt (3 °L):	4 oz (113 g)	4 oz (113 g)	1.6 lb (0.73 kg)
Crystal malt (60 °L):	6 oz (170 g)	6 oz (170 g)	2.3 lb (1.0 kg)
Pale malt syrup:	——	5 lb (2.3 kg)	——
Bittering hops			
Cluster (7% alpha):	1.3 oz (37 g)	1.3 oz (37 g)	6.7 oz (190 g)
HBU:	9	9	47
IBU:	34	34	34
Aroma hops			
Cascades (dry hop):	0.75 oz (21 g)	0.75 oz (21 g)	4.5 oz (128 g)
Color (°L):	~9	~9	~8

Water treatment:	Calcium 120 ppm; Sulfate 350 ppm; Chloride 40 ppm.
Mash temperature:	151°–153° F (66.1°–67.2° C)
Original gravity:	1.044 (10.9 °P)
Finishing gravity:	1.010–1.012 (2.5–3.0 °P)
Priming sugar:	1.5–2.0 oz (43–57 g) cane sugar, as syrup, in 5 gallons.
CO_2 (volumes):	0.8–1.2
Packaging:	Draught, but bottle if you must.

Note: In the extract brew, mix all three grains with four pints of water at about 160 degrees F (71 degrees C). Keep at around 155 degrees F (68 degrees C) for 45 to 60 minutes. Strain off grain, sparge with two quarts hot water and add liquid to main brew.

TANK IT DOWN ORDINARY BITTER

Amount	5 gallons (Grain)	5 gallons (Extract)	1 barrel (Grain)
British pale malt (2.5 °L):	4.3 lb (2.0 kg)	——	22.7 lb (10.3 kg)
Crystal malt (80 °L):	8 oz (227 g)	8 oz (227 g)	3.1 lb (1.4 kg)
Pale malt syrup:	——	4.1 lb (1.9 kg)	——
Flaked maize:	8 oz (227 g)	——	3.1 lb (1.4 kg)
Corn sugar:	8 oz (227 g)	10 oz (280 g)	3.1 lb (1.4 kg)
Color (°L):	~12	~12	~11
Bittering hops			
Bullion (9% alpha):	0.6 oz (17 g)	0.6 oz (17 g)	3.1 oz (88 g)
HBU:	5.4	5.4	28
IBU:	20	20	20
Aroma hops			
Goldings (dry hop):	1 oz (28 g)	1 oz (28 g)	6 oz (170 g)

Water treatment:	Calcium 100 ppm; Sulfate 300 ppm; Chloride 40 ppm.
Mash temperature:	150°–151° F (65.6°–66.1° C)
Original gravity:	1.035 (8.7 °P)
Finishing gravity:	1.007–1.009 (1.75–2.25 °P)
Priming sugar:	1.5 oz (43 g) cane sugar, as syrup, in 5 gallons.
CO_2 (volumes):	0.7–1
Packaging:	Draught, for quick drinking.

Note: In the extract brew, use the crystal malt as in Anglo-American Pale Ale. This is a good beer for a partial mash, adding one pound pale malt to the above recipe.

CLASSIC INDIA PALE ALE

Amount	5 gallons (Grain)	5 gallons (Extract)	1 barrel (Grain)
British pale			
malt (2.5 °L):	9.2 lb (4.2 kg)	2 lb (0.9 kg)	48.7 lb (22.1 kg)
Crystal malt (60 °L):	2 oz (57 g)	2 oz (57 g)	0.8 lb (360 g)
Pale malt syrup:	——	6 lb (2.7 kg)	——
Pale dry extract:	——	0.4 lb (180 g)	——
Color (°L):	~7	~7	~6
Bittering hops			
Goldings (5% alpha):	2.7 oz (77 g)	2.7 oz (77 g)	14 oz (397 g)
HBU:	13.5	13.5	70
IBU:	50.6	50.6	50.7
Aroma hops			
Goldings			
(end of boil):	1 oz (28 g)	1 oz (28 g)	6 oz (170 g)

Water treatment:	Calcium 200 ppm; Sulfate 500 ppm; Chloride 40 ppm.
Mash temperature:	152°–154° F (66.7°–67.8° C)
Original gravity:	1.055 (13.5 °P)
Finishing gravity:	1.012–1.014 (3.0–3.5 °P)
Priming sugar:	3 oz (85 g) cane sugar, as syrup, in 5 gallons.
CO_2 (volumes):	1.5–2.0
Packaging:	In bottle; also in keg, with two ounces priming sugar.

Note: In the extract brew the pale and crystal malts should be mashed, as in Pride of Milford Bitter.

"WEST" INDIA PALE ALE

Amount	5 gallons (Grain)	5 gallons (Extract)	1 barrel (Grain)
British pale malt (2.5 °L):	8.5 lb (3.9 kg)	2 lb (0.9 kg)	45.4 lb (20.6 kg)
Crystal malt (20 °L):	8 oz (227 g)	8 oz (227 g)	3.1 lb (1.4 kg)
Pale malt syrup:	——	6 lb (2.7 kg)	——
Bittering hops			
Galena (12% alpha):	1 oz (28 g)	1 oz (28 g)	5.2 oz (147 g)
HBU:	12	12	62
IBU:	45	45	45
Aroma hops			
Tettnanger (20 mins):	0.25 oz (7 g)	0.25 oz (7 g)	1.5 oz (43 g)
Fuggles (10 mins):	0.25 oz (7 g)	0.25 oz (7 g)	1.5 oz (43 g)
Cascades (end of boil):	0.5 oz (14 g)	0.5 oz (14 g)	3 oz (85 g)
Color (°L):	~8	~8	~7

Water treatment:	Calcium 170 ppm; Sulfate 400 ppm; Chloride 40 ppm.
Mash temperature:	151° 153° F (66.1°–67.2° C)
Original gravity:	1.054 (13.24 °P)
Finishing gravity:	1.012–1.014 (3.0–3.5 °P)
Priming sugar:	3 oz (85 g) cane sugar, as syrup, in 5 gallons.
CO_2 (volumes):	1.5–2.0
Packaging:	In bottle.

Note: In the extract brew the pale and crystal malts should be mashed, as in Pride of Milford Bitter.

117

350TH ANNIVERSARY INDIA PALE ALE

Amount	5 gallons (Grain)	5 gallons (Extract)	1 barrel (Grain)
British pale malt (2.5 °L):8 lb (3.6 kg)		2 lb (0.9 kg)	42.5 lb. (19.3 kg)
Crystal malt (40 °L): 6 oz. (170 g)		6 oz (170 g)	2.3 lb (1.0 kg)
Pale malt syrup: —		5.6 lb (2.5 kg)	—
Bittering hops			
Brewer's Gold (9% alpha):		1.4 oz (40 g)	1.4 oz (40 g)
7.4 oz. (210 g)			
HBU:	12.6	12.6	66.6
IBU:	47	47	48
Aroma hops			
Hallertauer (end of boil):		0.5 oz (14 g)	0.5 oz (14 g)
3 oz. (85 g)			
Talisman (dry-hop):	0.75 oz (21 g)	0,75 oz (21 g)	4.5 oz (128 g)
Color (°L):	~8	~8	~7

Water treatment:	Calcium 150 ppm; Sulfate 350 ppm; Chloride 40 ppm.
Mash temperature:	150°–152° F (65.6°–66.7° C)
Original gravity:	1.050 (12.3 °P)
Finishing gravity:	1.011–1.013 (2.75–3.25 °P)
Priming sugar:	1.5–2 oz (43–57 g) cane sugar, as syrup, in 5 gallons.
CO_2 (volumes):	0.8–1.2
Packaging:	Draught.

Note: In the extract brew the pale and crystal malts should be mashed, as in Pride of Milford Bitter.

FLAVOR NOTES ON RECIPE BEERS

1. Standard Pale Ale

A medium-gravity pale ale with low crystal-malt content. The relatively high sulfate level gives this beer a dryness which helps show off the classic Goldings hop bitterness and aroma to good advantage.

2. Beyond the Pale Pale Ale

A slightly higher-gravity beer with a little extra light-colored crystal malt to accentuate mouth feel without darkening the beer. Higher sulfate prevents extra malti-ness from masking the bitterness or the mixed spicy and flowery characters of the two aroma hops.

3. Anglo-American Pale Ale

At the lower end of pale ale's gravity specification, with correspondingly less bitterness. Still moderately high salt content so that bitterness comes through. A little extra dark-crystal malt adds color and mouth feel. The combination of hops accounts for the name, with the Goldings dry hopping adding a pungency lacking in the other two beers, making this a fine draught beer.

4. Yer Averidge Bitter

The name says it. Brewed at standard English gravity, with marked bitterness and without a compensating hop aroma. Extra crystal gives this thinnish, draught beer a little more body.

5. Pride of Milford Bitter

High in gravity for a bitter, with moderately high salt content to let the high bitterness come through the extra maltiness of high crystal-malt level. Good, flowery aroma

119

of Cascades, dry-hopped to increase complexity of the beer. A little wheat malt gives excellent head retention in this low-carbonated draught beer. As a high-quality bitter, the extract brew benefits from a partial mash approach.

6. Tank it Down Ordinary Bitter

A low-gravity brew, exemplifying the use of flaked maize and sugar. These adjuncts make for a thin brew, so plenty of dark crystal is there to give some mouth feel and color. A large amount of Goldings is dry-hopped to give the beer some much-needed character. Definitely a session beer to be drunk by the English pint!

7. Classic India Pale Ale

Top-of-the-line gravity, with very high sulfate to accentuate the very high hop acidity. Good Goldings character to improve depth and only a little crystal malt, to keep color pale. As with all three IPAs, the extract brew is improved by the partial-mash technique. A beer for slow, reflective drinking.

8. "West" India Pale Ale

Also a high-gravity brew, but with a little less sulfate and bitterness. The higher amount of pale crystal malt further softens the flavor. Mouth feel is increased, but color is kept down. Gets its name from use of several American hop varieties; the use of three different aroma hops gives it great aromatic complexity. A powerful, yet intriguing and subtle beer.

9. 350th Anniversary India Pale Ale

A slightly lower-gravity IPA, with good bitterness somewhat offset by moderate sulfate and a fairly large amount of medium-color crystal. The combination of spicy and resiny aroma hops gives this brew surprising impact, which makes it best served as a low-carbonated draught beer. The name comes from Milford's age. What better way could there be to celebrate such an important birthday?

COMMERCIAL EXAMPLES OF PALE ALE

I have a problem with this section. After all, because of the nature of the beer, we have to list English examples of the genre. This may not be terribly useful to an American drinker, especially as some of those imported into the United States have been tempered in flavor, supposedly to meet American taste. But there is no choice; *it is* an English brew.

I shall therefore list what I consider the best of the English brews available in the United States, although such availability is variable, particularly where the smaller traditional brewers are concerned. But since much of this beer is best on draught, I have to recommend at least some of my favorites that are not on sale in the United States. Perhaps that will inspire some readers to visit Britain and sample these beers on their home ground. Even better, perhaps it will inspire some state-side entrepreneur to bring real ale over to his country.

Luckily, there are now some excellent examples of U.S. pale ale, and I shall cover some of those I have liked best. However, the U.S. microbrewing industry has expanded so quickly that it is impossible to be up-to-date on everything available in such a big country. Therefore, my listing inevitably omits some excellent beers. Only beers which I have sampled on several occasions will be listed. The listing is a purely personal one and is definitely not intended to discourage you from sampling any other pale ale you may come across!

~ U.S. Pale Ales~

Ballantine India Pale Ale—Falstaff Brewery, Fort Wayne, Indiana. The Newark-brewed example was a copy of an original IPA recipe. It had all the ingredients of intense bitterness and hop aroma, plus an oaky flavor due to maturation in the North American variety of the wood. The Fort Wayne version does not seem to be so interesting, but is still worth trying.

Boston's Best Burton Bitter—Commonwealth Brewing Company, Boston, Massachusettes. Perhaps a little low on bitterness for my taste, but how could I resist including a beer with this name, especially when it is drawn by handpump?

Catamount Amber—Catamount Brewing Company, White River Junction, Vermont. A very sound version of this beer, made from U.S. ingredients, with perfect color and nice bitterness. I helped one of the partners get into brewing, so I'd better not say anymore!

India Pale Ale—Yakima Brewing and Malting Company, Yakima, Washington. Distinguished by being a draught beer, and by the use of U.S. hops to give a truly bitter example of the style. The brewer, Bert Grant, is technical director for a hop-grower and merchant—need I say more?

Liberty Ale—Anchor Brewing Company, San Francisco, California. I had to mention Anchor because it is one of my favorites, and this is such a splendidly hoppy pale ale it had to make the list. If this does not exemplify a fine pale ale, I don't know what does.

Pyramid Pale Ale—Hart Brewing, Kalama, Washington. Excellent on both bitterness and hop aroma (Cascades). Full of intrigue, it makes you keep wanting to come back and try to identify every flavor note. There may be others as good as this, but it's difficult to think of anything better.

Sierra Nevada Pale Ale—Sierra Nevada Brewing Company, Chico, California. Bottle-conditioned, with hops pouring out from it at every angle. Delightfully refreshing, yet complex and subtle, both the beer and the brewery should be an inspiration to anyone opening their own micro. I think this is my favorite.

- English Pale Ales in North America -

Bass Pale Ale—Still labelled "IPA," in a traditionally shaped bottle. Not a bad maltiness, but nowhere near as hoppy as it ought to be.

Fuller's London Pride—Perhaps not at its best in a bottle, but still a fine, hoppy example of the style, with good aroma as well as bitterness.

Royal Oak—Eldridge, Pope, Dorchester, Dorset. Less bitterness than I would like, but nicely malty. Probably fairly close to the original "country bitters."

Samuel Smith's Pale Ale—Brewed in Tadcaster, North Yorkshire, and often with a typical diacetyl "buttery" note. An excellent, authentic pale ale, worth looking for, except for its exorbitant price!

Young's Special London Ale—Brewed by Young's in Wandsworth, South London (where I grew up). Limited availability in the Northeast, which is a pity because this is a beer that really tells you how a pale ale should be hopped. A high-gravity pale ale (1.062 or 15.2 °P), but the hop flavor still tells it all!

- English Pale Ales -

Worthington White Shield—Bass Brewing, Burton-on-Trent, Staffordshire. Mentioned first because it is the only surviving English bottle-conditioned pale ale. Still a classic, with both hop and malt contributions. Unfortunately, and ironically, it does not seem to travel well, and samples drunk in the United States are often disappointing.

Adnam's Bitter—Adnam's, Southwold, Suffolk. A unique draught bitter, sometimes described as having a "seaweed" flavor.

Abbot Ale—Greene, King, Bury St. Edmunds, Suffolk. A fine pale ale, with excellent bitterness, all too often spoilt by excessive carbonation through "top-pressure" carbon-dioxide dispense.

ESB, and London Pride—Fuller, Smith and Turner, Chiswick, West London. Both beautiful examples of draught bitter, London Pride having a more noticeable bitterness and hop aroma, which is masked in the maltier, much stronger ESB. Don't miss them if you visit England!

124

Brewkettle at Paine's Brewery, St. Neots, Cambridgeshire.

Holt's Bitter—Holt, Manchester, Lancashire. A modest name for an average-gravity bitter with outstanding character. This is a beer that deserves much more recognition than it has outside of the brewery's trading area.

Hook Norton Best Bitter—Hook Norton Brewery, Hook Norton, Oxfordshire. A magnificent example of how to pack both bitterness and body into a low-gravity bitter.

Ind Coope Burton Ale—Ind Coope Burton Brewery, Burton-on-Trent, Staffordshire. A very malty, yet hoppy brew from the famous pale ale area. A demonstration that big brewers can brew beers of outstanding character if they want to!

Pedigree—Marston's, Burton-on-Trent, Staffordshire. The one remaining brewery still using Burton Unions.

The full flavor of this brew makes you wonder why Bass ever gave up this method of brewing.

Master Brew Bitter—Shepherd Neame, Faversham, Kent. A low-gravity beer with a distinctive hop bitterness, as befits the one remaining English brewer in England's premier hop-growing area.

Old Brewery Bitter—Samuel Smith, Tadcaster, North Yorkshire. All the character of the bottled pale ale, but the malt and diacetyl notes are unobscured by high carbonation.

Taylor's Landlord—Taylor's Brewery, Keighley, West Yorkshire. A sweetish bitter with a full, nutty flavor, quite unlike that of any other bitter.

Wadworth 6X—Wadworth's, Devizes, Wiltshire. A fine, malty, chewy brew; "country bitter" at its best.

Young's Special and Bitter—Young's Brewery, Wandsworth, South London. The bitter has a flavor to match its name, while the splendid Special reflects its higher gravity in an added maltiness. The Special is probably my all-time favorite draught bitter, but I'm not sure how much nostalgia has affected my judgment in this case!

If you want to know more about England's beers, Michael Jackson's *New World Guide to Beer* is required reading. If you plan on going to England to sample them, get a copy of CAMRA's current *Good Beer Guide* (Campaign For Real Ale, 34, Alma Road, St. Albans, Herts, AL1 3BW, England), and use it when planning your itinerary.

Glossary

adjunct. Any *unmalted* grain or other fermentable ingredient added to the mash.

aeration. The action of introducing air to the wort at various stages of the brewing process.

airlock. (see fermentation lock)

airspace. (see ullage)

alcohol by volume (v/v). The percentage of volume of alcohol per volume of beer. To calculate the approximate volumetric alcohol content, subtract the terminal gravity from the original gravity and divide the result by 75. For example: 1.050 – 1.012 – .038 / 75 = 5% v/v.

alcohol by weight. The percentage weight of alcohol per volume of beer. For example: 3.2% alcohol by weight = 3.2 grams of alcohol per 100 centiliters of beer.

ale. 1. Historically, a nonhopped malt beverage. 2. Now a generic term for hopped beers produced by top fermentation, as opposed to lagers, which are produced by bottom fermentation.

all-extract beer. A beer made with only malt extract as opposed to one made from barley, or a combination of malt extract and barley.

all-grain beer. A beer made with only malted barley as opposed to one made from malt extract, or from malt extract and malted barley.

127

all-malt beer. A beer made with only barley malt with no adjuncts or refined sugars.

alpha acid. A soft resin in hop cones. When boiled, alpha acids are connected to iso-alpha-acids, which account for 60 percent of a beer's bitterness.

alpha-acid unit. A measurement of the potential bitterness of hops, expressed by their percentage of alpha acid. Low = 2 to 4%, medium = 5 to 7%, high = 8 to 12%. Abbrev: A.A.U.

attenuation. The reduction in the wort's specific gravity caused by the transformation of sugars into alcohol and carbon-dioxide gas.

Balling. A saccharometer invented by Carl Joseph Napoleon Balling in 1843. It is calibrated for 63.5 degrees F (17.5 degrees C), and graduated in grams per hundred, giving a direct reading of the percentage of extract by weight per 100 grams solution. For example: 10 °B = 10 grams of sugar per 100 grams of wort.

blow-by (blow-off). A single-stage homebrewing fermentation method in which a plastic tube is fitted into the mouth of a carboy, with the other end submerged in a pail of sterile water. Unwanted residues and carbon dioxide are expelled through the tube, while air is prevented from coming into contact with the fermenting beer, thus avoiding contamination.

carbonation. The process of introducing carbon-dioxide gas into a liquid by: 1. injecting the finished beer with carbon dioxide; 2. adding young fermenting beer to finished beer for a renewed fermentation (kraeusening); 3. priming (adding sugar) to fermented wort prior to bottling, creating a secondary fermentation in the bottle.

carboy. A large glass, plastic or earthenware bottle.

chill haze. Haziness caused by protein and tannin during the secondary fermentation.

dry hopping. The addition of hops to the primary fermenter, the secondary fermenter, or to casked beer to add aroma and hop character to the finished beer without adding significant bitterness.

dry malt. Malt extract in powdered form.

extract. The amount of dissolved materials in the wort after mashing and lautering malted barley and/or malt adjuncts such as corn and rice.

fermentation lock. A one-way valve, which allows carbon-dioxide gas to escape from the fermenter while excluding contaminants.

final specific gravity. The specific gravity of a beer when fermentation is complete.

fining. The process of adding clarifying agents to beer during secondary fermentation to precipitate suspended matter.

flocculation. The behaviour in which yeast cells join into masses and settle out toward the end of fermentation.

homebrew bittering units. A formula invented by the American Homebrewers Association to measure bitterness of beer. Example: 1.5 ounces of hops at 10 percent alpha acid for five gallons: 1.5 x 10 = 15 HBU per five gallons.

hop pellets. Finely powdered hop cones compressed into tablets. Hop pellets are 20 to 30 percent stronger by weight than the same variety in loose form.

hydrometer. A glass instrument used to measure the specific gravity of liquids as compared to water, consisting of a graduated stem resting on a weighed float.

International bitterness units. An approximate (within 20%) method of measuring bitterness in beer based on parts per million content of alpha acids. IBUs are calculated with the following formula:

$$B.U. = \frac{H \times (a\text{-}a + b\ a/9)}{0.3}$$

where: H = weight of hops in grams per liter (H g/l)
a-a = alpha acid percent
b-a = beta acid percent

isinglass. A gelatinous substance made from the swim bladder of certain fish and added to beer as a fining agent.

kraeusen. (n.) The rocky head of foam which appears on the surface of the wort during fermentation. (v.) Adding fermenting wort to fermented beer to induce carbonation through a secondary fermentation.

lager. (n.) A generic term for any bottom-fermented beer. Lager brewing is now the predominant brewing method worldwide except in Britain where top fermented ales dominate. (v.) Storing beer at near-zero temperatures to precipitate yeast cells and proteins and improve taste.

lauter tun. A vessel with a false, slotted bottom and spigot in which the mash settles and the grains are removed from the sweet wort through a straining process.

liquefaction. The process by which alpha-amylase enzymes degrade soluble starch into dextrin.

malt. Barley that has been steeped in water, germinated and dried in kilns to convert insoluble starchs to soluble substances and sugars.

malt extract. A thick syrup or dry powder prepared from malt.

mashing. Mixing ground malt with water to extract the fermentables, degrade haze-forming proteins and convert grain starches to fermentable sugars and nonfermentable carbohydrates.

modification. 1. The physical and chemical changes in barley as a result of malting. 2. The degree to which these changes have occured, as determined by the growth of the acrospire.

original gravity. The specific gravity of wort previous to fermentation and compared to the density of water at 39.2 degrees F (4 degrees C), which is given the value 1.000. A measure of the total amount of dissolved solids in wort.

pH. Potential of hydrogen. A measure of acidity or alkalinity of a solution, usually on a scale of one to 14, where seven is neutral.

Plato. A saccharometer which expresses specific gravity as extract weight in a one-hundred-gram solution at 64 degrees F (18 degrees C). A revised, more accurate version of Balling, by Dr. Plato.

primary fermentation. The first stage of fermentation, during which most fermentable sugars are converted to ethyl alcohol and carbon dioxide.

priming sugar. A small amount of corn, malt or cane sugar added to bulk beer prior to racking or at bottling to induce a new fermentation and create carbonation.

racking. The process of transferring beer from one container to another, especially into the final package (bottles, kegs, etc.).

Reinheitsgebot. A German purity law governing the production of beer. It states that only water, malted barley, malted wheat and hops can be used to make beer.

saccharification. The naturally occurring process in which malt starch is converted into fermentable sugars, primarily maltose.

saccharometer. An instrument that determines the sugar concentration of a solution by measuring the specific gravity.

secondary fermentation. 1. The second, slower stage of fermentation, lasting from a few weeks to many months depending on the type of beer. 2. A fermentation occuring in bottles or casks and initiated by priming or adding yeast.

sparging. Spraying the spent grains in the mash with hot water to retrieve the remaining malt sugar.

specific gravity. A measure of a substance's density as compared to that of water, which is given the value of 1.000 at 39.2 degrees F (4 degrees C). Specific gravity is dimensionless, with no accompanying units, because it is expressed as a ratio.

starter. A batch of fermenting yeast, added to the wort to initiate fermentation.

strike temperature. The initial temperature of the water when the malted barley is added to it to create the mash.

tied house. In England, a system by which a pub or inn is tied to a single brewery, usually through a debt owed, and serves its beer according to a financially based agreement.

trub. Suspended particles resulting from the precipitation of proteins, hop oils and tannins during boiling and cooling stages of brewing.

ullage. The empty space between a liquid and the top of its container. Also called airspace or headspace.

water hardness. The degree of dissolved minerals in water.

wort. The mixture that results from mashing the malt and boiling the hops, before it is fermented into beer.

Index

134

HOMEBREWER?

Join the thousands of American Homebrewers Association members who read **zymurgy** — the magazine for homebrewers and beer lovers.

Every issue of **zymurgy** is full of tips, techniques, new recipes, new products, equipment and ingredient reviews, beer news, technical articles — the whole world of homebrewing. PLUS, the AHA brings members the National Homebrewers Conference, the National Homebrew Competition, the Beer Judge Certification Program, the Homebrew Club Network, periodic discounts on books from Brewers Publications and much, much more.

Photocopy and mail this coupon today to join the AHA or call now for credit card orders, (303) 546-6514.

- -

Name

Address

City   State/Province

Zip/Postal Code   Country

Phone

☐ Enclosed is $29 for one full year.
Canadian memberships are $34 U.S., Foreign memberships are $44 U.S.

☐ Please charge my credit card ☐ Visa ☐ MC

Card No.   —   —   —   Exp. Date

Signature

Make check to: American Homebrewers Association, PO Box 1510, Boulder, CO 80306 USA
Offer valid until 12/31/95.   Prices subject to change.   PA94

BOOKS for Brewers and Beer Lovers

Order Now ... Your Brew Will Thank You!

These books offered by Brewers Publications are some of the most sought after reference tools for homebrewers and professional brewers alike. Filled with tips, techniques, recipes and history, these books will help you expand your brewing horizons. Let the world's foremost brewers help you as you brew. Whatever your brewing level or interest, Brewers Publications has the information necessary for you to brew the best beer in the world — your beer.

Please send me more free information on the following: (check all that apply)

◊ Merchandise & Book Catalog ◊ Institute for Brewing Studies
◊ American Homebrewers Association ◊ Great American Beer Festival℠

Ship to:

Name

Address

City   State/Province

Zip/Postal Code   Country

Daytime Phone (   )

Please use the following in conjunction with order form when ordering books from Brewers Publications.

Payment Method

◊ Check or Money Order Enclosed (Payable to the Association of Brewers)
◊ Visa   ◊ MasterCard

Card Number   –   –   Expiration Date

Name on Card   Signature

Brewers Publications Inc., PO Box 1510, Boulder, CO 80306-1510; (303) 546-6514, FAX (303) 447-2825.
PA94

BREWERS PUBLICATIONS ORDER FORM

PROFESSIONAL BREWING BOOKS

QTY.	TITLE	STOCK #	PRICE	EXT. PRICE
_____	Brewery Planner	500	80.00	_____
_____	North American Brewers Resource Directory	504	80.00	_____
_____	Principles of Brewing Science	463	29.95	_____

THE BREWERY OPERATIONS SERIES
from Micro and Pubbrewers Conferenooo

QTY.	TITLE	STOCK #	PRICE	EXT. PRICE
_____	Volume 6, 1989 Conference	536	25.95	_____
_____	Volume 7, 1990 Conference	537	25.95	_____
_____	Volume 8, 1991 Conference, Brewing Under Adversity	538	25.95	_____
_____	Volume 9, 1992 Conference, Quality Brewing — Share the Experience	539	25.95	_____

CLASSIC BEER STYLE SERIES

QTY.	TITLE	STOCK #	PRICE	EXT. PRICE
_____	Pale Ale	401	11.95	_____
_____	Continental Pilsener	402	11.95	_____
_____	Lambic	403	11.95	_____
_____	Vienna, Märzen, Oktoberfest	404	11.95	_____
_____	Porter	405	11.95	_____
_____	Belgian Ale	406	11.95	_____
_____	German Wheat Beer	407	11.95	_____
_____	Scotch Ale	408	11.95	_____
_____	Bock	409	11.95	_____

BEER AND BREWING SERIES, for homebrewers and beer enthusiasts,
from National Homebrewers Conferences

QTY.	TITLE	STOCK #	PRICE	EXT. PRICE
_____	Volume 8, 1988 Conference	448	21.95	_____
_____	Volume 10, 1990 Conference, Brew Free Or Die!	450	21.95	_____
_____	Volume 11, 1991 Conference, Brew Free Or Die!	451	21.95	_____
_____	Volume 12, 1992 Conference, Just Brew It!	452	21.95	_____

GENERAL BEER AND BREWING INFORMATION

QTY.	TITLE	STOCK #	PRICE	EXT. PRICE
_____	The Art of Cidermaking (Available in May 1995)	468	14.95	_____
_____	Brewing Lager Beer	460	14.95	_____
_____	Brewing Mead	461	11.95	_____
_____	Dictionary of Beer and Brewing	462	19.95	_____
_____	Evaluating Beer	465	19.95	_____
_____	Great American Beer Cookbook	466	24.95	_____
_____	Victory Beer Recipes	467	11.95	_____
_____	Winners Circle	464	11.95	_____

—————————————————————**SUBTOTAL** _____

Call or write for a free *Beer Enthusiast* catalog today.
• U.S. funds only.
• All Brewers Publications books come with a money-back guarantee.
*Postage & Handling: $4 for the first book ordered, plus $1 for each book thereafter. Canadian and foreign orders please add $5 for the first book and $2 for each book thereafter. Orders cannot be shipped without appropriate P&H.

Colo. Residents Add
3% Sales Tax _____
P & H * _____
TOTAL _____

Brewers Publications Inc., PO Box 1510, Boulder, CO 80306-1510; (303) 546-6514, FAX (303) 447-2825.

PA94

Examine the World of
Microbrewing
and
Pubbrewing

Travel the world of commercial, small-scale brewing; the realm of microbrewers and pubbrewers.

No Risk Offer

Subscribe now and receive six issues. Money-back guarantee

The New Brewer magazine guides you through this new industry. Its pages introduce you to marketing, finance, operations, equipment, recipes, interviews — in short, the whole landscape.

Subscribe to *The New Brewer* and become a seasoned traveler.

$55 a year (U.S.)
$65 (Foreign)
U.S. funds only

Published by the Institute for Brewing Studies, PO Box 1510, Boulder, CO 80306-1510; (303) 546-6514.

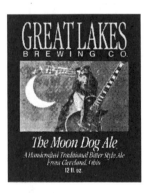

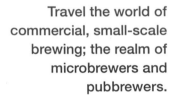

The New Brewer
THE MAGAZINE FOR MICRO- AND PUB-BREWERS